CURANDEREANDO

LANI CUPCHOY

CURANDEREANDO

Sacred Decolonial Healing

THE UNIVERSITY OF
ARIZONA PRESS
TUCSON

The University of Arizona Press
www.uapress.arizona.edu

We respectfully acknowledge the University of Arizona is on the land and territories of Indigenous peoples. Today, Arizona is home to twenty-two federally recognized tribes, with Tucson being home to the O'odham and the Yaqui. The university strives to build sustainable relationships with sovereign Native Nations and Indigenous communities through education offerings, partnerships, and community service.

ISBN-13: 978-0-8165-5755-4 (hardcover)
ISBN-13: 978-0-8165-5754-7 (paperback)
ISBN-13: 978-0-8165-5756-1 (ebook)

Cover design by Leigh McDonald
Cover art by Lani Cupchoy
Designed and typeset by Leigh McDonald in Calluna 10.5/14 and Dragoo WF (display)

Publication of this book is made possible in part by the proceeds of a permanent endowment created with the assistance of a Challenge Grant from the National Endowment for the Humanities, a federal agency.

Library of Congress Cataloging-in-Publication Data
Names: Cupchoy, Lani, 1977– author
Title: Curandereando : sacred decolonial healing / Lani Cupchoy.
Description: Tucson : University of Arizona Press, 2026. | Includes bibliographical references and index.
Identifiers: LCCN 2026004876 (print) | LCCN 2026004877 (ebook) | ISBN 9780816557554 hardcover | ISBN 9780816557547 paperback | ISBN 9780816557561 ebook
Subjects: LCSH: Traditional medicine—Philosophy | Healing—Philosophy
Classification: LCC GN477 .C86 2026 (print) | LCC GN477 (ebook) | DDC 610.1—dc23/eng/20260401
LC record available at https://lccn.loc.gov/2026004876
LC ebook record available at https://lccn.loc.gov/2026004877

Printed in the United States of America
♾ This paper meets the requirements of ANSI/NISO Z39.48-1992 (Permanence of Paper).

CONTENTS

CONTENTS

PREFATORY INVOCACIÓN

The first time I met Dra. Lani Cupchoy was in the context of academia. Dra. Cupchoy was a visiting professor at Pitzer College and part of the Intercollegiate Department of Chicana/o Latina/o Studies in Claremont, California. As visiting faculty, the courses Dra. Cupchoy conducted were always inspiring, and she quickly became a favorite among students. To my great fortune, I was able to interact with Dra. Cupchoy early in her teaching at Pitzer College for the Latina Activism, Work and Protest course when she invited me to speak. As I walked into the classroom, the energy and the welcoming space Dra. Cupchoy had created throughout the course were palpable. A sense of calm and assurance permeated the room, and I knew from the energy alone that she was an amazing and inclusive instructor. I led a workshop that day where we were able to participate and interact in ways we had not before. Later I discovered that she was also a singer and songwriter, and it all made sense. One can gauge the effectiveness of an instructor by students' recommendations, and her students always came away feeling transformed. It seemed to me that Dra. Cupchoy's way of integrating music, art, and culture as a method was an essential part of her value system, and it was then that I knew we had a lot in common. We have been in correspondence ever since. When she asked me to write an invocation for this book, I jumped at the chance.

Curanderismo is a practice of traditional healing that involves the earth's remedies and rituals, which encompass the material and the spiritual realms. As Dra. Cupchoy expresses in this book, "It is a worldview, a way of being that sees the earth as sacred, the spirit as central, and the community as intertwined."

Through personal accounts, poetry, oral history, historical research, and, of course, an undying commitment to community and social justice, Dra. Cupchoy has made the most remarkable offering. Rooted in an Indigenous, African, and European acknowledgment of the roots of curanderismo, this book is an interdisciplinary ride through an understanding of the practice as an interconnected world legacy and a decolonial tool. Dra. Cupchoy navigates many voices in consolidating this important offering—the voice of history, the voice of analysis, and the voice of poetic prose. Intertwined, they weave "the fabric of healing and resilience for future generations."

However, what inspired me the most is her artist voice and the ways in which her poetry captures the spirit and resilient nature of curanderismo. An artist like Dra. Cupchoy might indeed be the best person to describe these ancient practices and connect them within and across national borders, for she has felt them in the body and expressed them through her artistic and poetic practice.

As you will witness, Dra. Cupchoy describes the true importance of the work of being a curandera then and now. You get a sense that to be a curandere and to enact curanderismo is not a static practice or something you study, but, as the book suggests, an action best expressed by a verb—*curandereando*—"A way of being. A way of life." She reminds us that many cultures have curanderes. Curanderes are in Mexico, the Andes, Guatemala, Africa, and Central and South America.

Furthermore, curanderes have existed as not only mujer-identified but also queer and gender-expansive practitioners. They indeed have existed and continue to actively resist olvido in the modern world and in the face of global and ecological challenges. *Curandereando* does more than inform us of the history and significance of curanderismo—it is an invitation and a healing remedy for the times.

We must learn these ancient ways. Know the remedies. Relearn the philosophy. The information is sacred, and in our learning, we are actively resisting a colonial mandate—el olvido. This work is a reminder that we must not lose hope in the face of American fascism, climate catastrophe, or ongoing genocides. As Dra. Cupchoy explains, we must listen to the earth and her spirit, for we have always had her healing remedies and the curanderes themselves. The learning and enactment of these ancient practices is a radical decolonial act that can offer solace and, ultimately, alivio.

Martha Gonzalez
Associate Professor
Intercollegiate Department of Chicana/o Latina/o Studies
Scripps/Claremont College

FOREWORD

¡La Lucha Sigue!

In her 2015 Goldman Prize speech, Berta Cáceres, the Hondureña feminist Indigenous activist, implored,

> Let us wake up! Let us wake up humanity! We are out of time. We must shake our conscience free of the rapacious capitalism, racism, and patriarchy that will only assure our self-destruction. . . . Our mother earth, militarized, fenced-in, poisoned, a place where basic rights are systematically violated, demands that we act. Let us build societies that can coexist in a dignified way, in a way that protects life. Let us come together and remain hopeful as we defend and care for the blood of this earth and its spirits.

Connecting capitalism, racism, patriarchy, and ongoing genocidal state violence in the Américas, Berta Cáceres calls on us to build a life-affirming world that prioritizes Mother Earth and its inhabitants over profits and violence.

For over five hundred years the structures and ideologies of European settler colonialism have wreaked havoc on working-class and campesino communities in the Américas. Indigenous populations saw their lands usurped, their labor stolen, and their knowledges and worldviews dismissed and often erased. Within decades of colonization, disease ravaged communities, leading to the death of between 85 and 95 percent of Indigenous people. In their efforts to extract wealth and impose their ways of life, colonizers participated in the kidnapping and enslavement of nearly thirteen million Africans. The genocidal impact of settler colonialism, capitalism, and patriarchy is evident in the policies and practices of the church, the state, and corporations to control land, the environment, production, labor, bodies, minds, and spirits.

Communities have persisted in a six-century-long struggle to maintain autonomy and keep themselves whole. Indigenous people resisted their invaders by rising up, defending themselves, negotiating and adapting, migrating away from European settlements, educating their youth, and finding strength in their deep histories, cultures, and communities. Africans who escaped their enslavers forged insurgent autonomous self-governing communities, quilombos and palenques, with Indigenous peoples and other rebels. Even as colonial violence fractured communities and states imposed languages and laws seeking to expunge Indigenous, African, and other traditional ways of knowing and being, these communities resisted and persisted.

As Dr. Lani Cupchoy powerfully demonstrates in *Curandereando: Sacred Decolonial Healing*, the struggle for holistic well-being continues with the work and knowledge of curanderas, community-based healers. Drawing from centuries of Afro-Indigenous ways of knowing, cosmologies, and experiences, curanderas are recentering relationships between humans, other sentient beings, the earth, the cosmos, the elements, and the spirits. Dr. Cupchoy challenges traditional Western academic approaches by blending testimonios and oral histories with poetic invocations to illustrate how curanderas address the social, cultural, and personal alienation at the core of settler colonialism. *Curandereando*, she emphasizes, evokes the active, transformative process of healing—through rituals, remedies, and spiritual connection. Rooted in Latin American traditions, this book highlights curanderismo's resilience: its survival under colonial oppression, its adaptations across diasporas, and its role in responding to today's ecological and social crises.

Dr. Cupchoy's approach is that of a "historian as curandera." As Aurora Levins Morales has demonstrated, a critical historian can function as a curandera, striving to heal the wounds of colonialism and patriarchy by uncovering the past and telling untold stories of women, Indigenous people, and others whose histories have been repressed. This is exactly what Dr. Cupchoy does. She is a holistic scholar who approaches research as relationship building. Dr. Cupchoy's starting point was her relationship with her grandmothers and the healing labor that they did in their communities. Her abuelas passed on this knowledge to Dr. Cupchoy and her mother. With that knowledge as a foundation, she conducted over thirty interviews and dialogues with curanderas from diverse backgrounds, regions, approaches, and generations.

Dr. Cupchoy's book challenges conventional ethnographic studies. She positions curanderismo as an active, decolonial force rather than just a subject of academic observation. Weaving the testimonios and stories of curanderas together with archival and secondary research throughout her text, she tells a story that reflects the creativity and adaptability of curanderas. Often existing outside the gaze of hegemonic institutions, curanderas are part of the glue of working-class and rural communities throughout Latin America as well as in immigrant communities in the United States. Because of this, Dr. Cupchoy recognizes that Western academic approaches to history, much like Western medicine for curanderas, are not the only or even the best approach. She introduces her chapters with poetic invocations that are narratives of resistance, pulling readers in and inviting us to be accomplices in her subversive telling of this history.

Enrique C. Ochoa
Professor of Latin American Studies and History
California State University at Los Angeles

PREFACE

Curanderismo is not merely a tradition you learn; it is a song the body remembers, an inheritance whispered through leaves, waters, and prayers. It lingers in the scent of copal curling into the air, in the soft murmur of hands breaking rue over weary bodies, and in the knowing eyes of those who have walked before us. This book is a vessel for that memory, a bridge built from fragments of ritual, poetry, and testimony to carry the unbroken spirit of curanderismo forward.

For decades, I have walked this path as a holistic practitioner, rooted in the wisdom of my abuela curanderas, yet continually shaped by the teachings of countless healers from across the world. Their guidance—spanning traditions as vast as the landscapes they inhabit—has revealed the sacred intersections of healing, resistance, and community. Curanderismo, as I have lived it, is not static; it adapts, evolves, and survives. It is both an ancient tradition and a revolutionary force, rooted in reciprocity, resilience, and the interconnectedness of body, mind, spirit, and earth.

Holistic healing is at the heart of curanderismo. It is not merely about curing ailments but about restoring harmony—between the physical and the spiritual, the individual and the collective, the human and the ecological. It is the tía who passes el huevo over a restless child, the abuela who offers a quiet "Drink this tecito," steeped in ancestral knowledge.

It is found in whispered prayers, quiet meditations, and the rituals we create to navigate life's fractures. These acts, often unnoticed, embody a profound truth: healing is not a singular act but a weaving of many threads, a reclamation of balance in a fragmented world.

This book moves beyond conventional views of curanderismo, tracing how it has been practiced across time and space—during the Inquisition, when healers were forced underground; across borders and migrations, where traditions were adapted to new landscapes; and into the diaspora, where curanderismo has taken on vibrant and evolving forms. It is a testament to how healing practices have endured, transformed, and reimagined themselves in the face of persecution, displacement, and cultural shifts. Today, curanderismo manifests in ways both rooted in ancestral wisdom and adapted to meet the needs of the present, reflecting its power as a living, breathing tradition.

This book is a counternarrative, a testament to the resilience of curanderas, curanderos, and curanderes who practiced in the shadows, resisting persecution by the Catholic Church, society, and even their own families. These healers, silenced but never extinguished, carried the wisdom of their ancestors underground, weaving it into survival. To write this book is to honor their defiance, to reclaim what colonization sought to erase, and to center their voices in a world still aching for their knowledge.

Curanderismo is decolonial and revolutionary; it is rooted in Indigenous knowledge and the radical act of remembering. It challenges systems that suppress the sacred and offers a vision grounded in balance, reciprocity, and reverence for the interconnectedness of all life. This book is not a history lesson or an ethnography; it is an invocation, an offering. It holds the aching beauty of resilience, the bold act of preserving wisdom through erasure. It is a song for those who braid the threads of past and present, healing not just the body but the land, the spirit, the collective.

Writing this has been like holding a shard of obsidian to sunlight: a moment of revelation, a reckoning with shadow, a communion with fire. It began in the stories that rooted me—stories shared by my abuelas over steaming pots of herbal tea, by strangers whose hands trembled with the weight of memory, and by the earth herself, who bore witness to it all.

Their voices, rising like wind through branches, shaped these pages into an altar where the sacred meets the everyday.

To write this is to say, "Aquí estamos"—we are still here. Still gathering herbs at dawn, still offering prayers at altars, still weaving survival into the fabric of the sacred. This book is my offering, a handful of wildflowers placed before the threshold of those who came before me and those who will come after. It is an invitation to walk this path with me, through memory and ritual, and to reclaim what was never truly lost.

May you find yourself in these pages—in the flicker of a candle, the brush of a healer's hand, the echo of ancestral voices calling you back to yourself. This is not just a book; for many, it is a remembering.

Lani Cupchoy

CURANDEREANDO

INTRODUCTION

The Call of the Curandera

This book begins, as all healing journeys do, with an invocation. It is a call to the ancestors, to the earth, and to the spirit within all of us—a reminder that healing is sacred work, rooted in both memory and presence. In exploring curanderismo, we honor the healers of the past while opening pathways for its evolution in the present and future. This is not just a study of tradition but an invitation to participate in its enduring legacy.

OPENING INVOCATION

Te llamo, hija de la tierra, hija de las estrellas,
para que recuerdes el poder que llevas en tu sangre.
Con mis manos recojo las hierbas; con mi corazón recojo las oraciones.
With my hands, I gather herbs; with my heart, I gather prayers.
Éste es el camino de nuestra gente—curar, recordar, resistir.
This is the way of our people—to heal, to remember, to resist.

Madre Tierra me guía, mis ancestros caminan conmigo.
Earth Mother guides me, my ancestors walk with me.
Escucha su voz en el viento, sus susurros en la lluvia.

Hear their voice in the wind, their whispers in the rain.
Te llamo, porque el mundo necesita sanar.
I call to you, because the world needs healing.

Hija del maíz, hija del sol,
ven a escuchar el susurro de las estrellas.
Con el fuego purifico, con el agua bendigo.
With fire, I purify; with water, I bless.

Somos las que sobreviven, las que recuerdan.
We are the ones who survive, the ones who remember.
Camina conmigo, porque la sanación es resistencia.
Walk with me, for healing is resistance.

Te llamo desde la raíz y el brote,
desde el fuego del volcán y la calma del río.
Escucha el canto del cenzontle, el llanto del copal.
Desde el amanecer del maíz hasta la sombra de la luna,
camina conmigo.

Through the roots and blossoms, I call you,
through the volcano's fire and the river's calm.
Hear the song of the cenzontle, the weeping of copal.
From the dawn of maize to the shadow of the moon,
walk with me.

RECLAIMING THE CURANDERA'S PLACE IN HISTORY

In 1612, a curandera named María was brought before the Inquisition in Mexico City, accused of "superstitious" practices. Her accusers feared her power, yet they also sought her remedies for their own ailments. María's story is one of many, revealing how curanderas navigated a world that sought to suppress them while secretly depending on their knowledge.

Beyond María, there were countless others—curanderas whose names were lost but whose voices echo through history. In Guatemala, the Maya healers resisted the Catholic Church's attempts to stamp out their practices, embedding their rituals in feast days and festivals. In the Andean highlands, the curanderas carried coca leaves and prayers up sacred mountains, weaving resilience into every step. Each act of healing was an act of defiance, a refusal to let the colonizer's narrative be the only one remembered.

For centuries, the curandera has lived on the edges of written history, dismissed as a figure of folklore or vilified as a bruja. Yet her hands have carried the knowledge of the earth, and her prayers have bridged the realms of the living and the divine. She is a healer, a spiritual guide, and a keeper of ancestral wisdom. Her remedies and rituals are rooted in practices older than colonization, deeper than memory.

The world has often sought to erase her voice, yet she remains. She exists in the shadows of colonial records as a heretic or witch, her knowledge feared and misunderstood. She exists in the whispered stories of families, the murmured prayers of those seeking protection, and the sacred smoke rising from altars. This book seeks to bring her voice into the light—not as a relic of the past, but as a vital force of healing and resistance.

Curanderismo, the practice of traditional healing, is not merely a set of remedies or rituals. It reflects a worldview, a way of being that sees the earth as sacred, the spirit as central, and the members of the community as intertwined. It draws from the interwoven spiritual practices of Indigenous peoples, including those of African and Native descent, as well as colonial European influences, and is born from a time when the land was medicine and the stars were guides. And it is deeply decolonial in its practice, a living resistance to the systems that sought to sever humanity from nature, spirit, and self.

This book centers the voice of the curandera, not as a silent figure observed from afar, but as an active participant in her own story. Through her eyes, we journey into the history, power, and resilience of curanderismo. Through her voice, we hear the call to heal not only our bodies but our histories and our futures.

While the term *curandera* traditionally refers to female healers, it is important to recognize the evolving nature of curanderismo. In its modern practice, healers may identify as curanderas, curanderos, or curanderes, reflecting the expansive and inclusive spirit of this tradition. This book uses "curandera" where historically accurate but embraces the broader spectrum of identities that shape curanderismo today.

This book contains a collection of testimonios that aim to honor the lives, wisdom, and resilience of curanderas across time and space. The term *testimonio* is used here to reflect both individual lived experiences and reconstructed narratives rooted in historical research, oral traditions, and ethnographic studies. Some of these stories are based on direct accounts, passed down through generations, while others are composite narratives created to represent broader realities and practices of curanderismo. In this work, testimonio is not merely a recounting of events but a way of being, a connection to ancestral knowledge, and a reclamation of voices often silenced or marginalized by colonial and modern narratives. Each story, whether drawn from historical record, taken from oral memory, or reconstructed from the fragments left behind, seeks to embody the spirit of curanderismo as both a sacred tradition and a practice of resistance. By weaving together these testimonios, this book aims to illuminate the enduring power of curanderas and the communities they serve. Their voices, rituals, and connections to the land remind us that healing is not just an individual act but a collective, ancestral, and revolutionary process. Through these pages, their stories live on.

PERSONAL CONNECTION: A MOTHER'S HEALING TOUCH

My first memory of healing is from when I was just two years old. I had fallen off my bicycle, landing hard on my knee. It swelled almost immediately, filling with water, and I could not walk without pain. My cries brought my mother running, and instead of reaching for ice or a bandage, she walked into the backyard, where the answers were waiting.

She returned with fresh aloe vera, arnica, and other herbs she knew by heart, each chosen for its healing properties. I watched as she carefully heated them, releasing their medicinal essence, and placed the warm mixture gently on my injured knee. Her hands moved with confidence and her words were calm, as though she were drawing on something ancient and unshakable. That night, as I slept, the swelling began to disappear, and by the next morning I could walk as if nothing had happened.

At the time, I did not understand the significance of what she had done. To me, it was just what mothers do—make the pain go away. But now I see how that moment held the essence of curanderismo: the intuitive knowledge of plants, the careful blending of remedies, and the belief in the body's ability to heal with the earth's help. My mother may not have called herself a curandera, but her hands carried the same wisdom passed down through generations.

As I grew older, I began to see how my mother's quiet acts of healing reflected something much larger—a lineage of knowledge passed down through generations. Her remedies were not just practical; they were spiritual, connecting us to a world where the earth itself was alive and responsive. It was not until I began studying curanderismo that I realized the power of what she carried and how her hands echoed the hands of curanderas across centuries. What began as a personal memory of my mother's hands grew into a journey of understanding—a recognition that her practices were part of a larger tradition of survival and wisdom. Scholars, poets, and activists have illuminated curanderismo's layers, revealing its power to heal not just individuals but histories, communities, and futures.

This book is an offering to my mother and to all who carry that spirit—to the women and fems who heal with their hands, their prayers, and their connection to the earth. It is a way to honor their legacy and bring their voices into the light. As I grew, the memory of my mother's quiet acts of healing became a touchstone—a reminder of the power rooted in the intertwining of the ordinary and the sacred. Her remedies, drawn from a lineage older than memory, sparked my curiosity and eventually my commitment to understanding the broader legacy of curanderas. This book is both a tribute and an offering, weaving personal reflection with the stories of countless healers whose voices continue to guide and inspire.

A LEGACY OF HEALING: SITUATING CURANDERISMO IN SCHOLARSHIP

Curanderismo, the traditional healing practice blending Indigenous, African, and European influences, is far more than a collection of remedies or rituals. It is a worldview—a philosophy rooted in connection to the land, body, and spirit. The curandera, as a healer and guide, embodies this practice through her role as a bridge between the sacred and the earthly. Scholars, poets, and practitioners have shed light on the complexity of curanderismo, tracing its history, evolution, and adaptability. This section explores what has been written about the curandera, identifies gaps in the literature, and situates this book within the field as a vital contribution to the ongoing legacy of curanderismo.

The historical and cultural dimensions of curanderismo have been richly examined, situating the practice within a legacy of resistance and survival. Patrisia Gonzales, in *Red Medicine: Traditional Indigenous Rites of Birthing and Healing*, not only engages deeply with the subject but also embodies the work she describes. A scholar-practitioner, Gonzales frames curanderismo within a larger continuum of Indigenous healing traditions, emphasizing its relationality to land and ancestors as a source of balance and restoration. Her work offers a lived, holistic understanding of curanderismo, blending scholarly insight with personal and cultural practice. The inclusion of her own perspective highlights the ways in which curanderismo is not just studied but lived and practiced as a means of survival, resistance, and restoration. Similarly, Brett Hendrickson, in "Curanderismo in the Americas," traces the historical evolution of curanderismo as a fusion of healing traditions from Indigenous, African, and European roots, offering a comprehensive view of its development across Latin America and the U.S. Southwest. Expanding this geographic scope, Maria Esmeralda Perez's MA thesis, "Curanderismo and Healing Rituals: An Ethnographic and Historical Study of the Casma Valley in Northern Peru," delves into the localized rituals and healing traditions that contribute to the diversity of curanderismo. Perez's work underscores the importance of examining curanderismo within its specific cultural and ecological contexts, revealing how practices in regions like the Casma Valley adapt to local needs while remaining deeply connected to broader Indigenous healing frameworks. This level of specificity provides a richer understanding of curanderismo as both a locally situated and a globally resonant tradition.

Beyond its historical foundations, curanderismo is also deeply tied to identity and acts of cultural resistance. Gloria Anzaldúa, in *Borderlands / La Frontera*, positions the curandera within the concept of the "borderlands," a space where physical, emotional, and spiritual worlds converge. She draws parallels between the curandera's work and nepantla, or in-between space, where identities are negotiated and survival becomes an act of resistance. Building on this framework, Aurora Levins Morales, in *Medicine Stories: Essays for Radicals*, portrays the curandera as a cultural historian and archivist whose healing preserves ancestral memory and counters the erasures of colonialism. For Morales, the curandera's work is inherently political, tied to liberation movements and communal healing.

The everyday realities of curanderismo have also been explored through practice-based and ethnographic studies that ground the tradition in lived experience. Eliseo "Cheo" Torres's *Curandero: A Life in Mexican Folk Healing* provides an intimate portrayal of curanderismo as practiced today, demystifying rituals such as limpias and herbal remedies while underscoring their accessibility and relevance. Meanwhile, Rainer W. Bussmann investigates the globalization of traditional medicine in "The Globalization of Traditional Medicine in Northern Peru," revealing how curanderismo has adapted to contemporary medical paradigms while retaining its spiritual essence.

In literature, storytelling has emerged as a powerful medium to explore the curandera's dual role as healer and keeper of communal memory. Sandra Cisneros, in her short story collection *Woman Hollering Creek*, uses fictional narratives to integrate the figure of the curandera as a symbol of resilience and spiritual guidance, emphasizing her ability to bridge personal and collective healing. Similarly, Cherríe Moraga's *Loving in the War Years* delves into the intersections of queerness, Chicana identity, and activism, presenting the curandera's work as a reclamation of community and self through love and resistance.

Beyond works based on storytelling, the spiritual and social hybridity of curanderismo is reflected in works that explore its blending of traditions. Theresa Delgadillo's *Spiritual Mestizaje* examines how curanderismo interweaves Indigenous, Catholic, and feminist elements, offering a vision of healing that adapts across borders and generations. Oral histories collected by Nasario García further capture the living traditions of curanderismo, documenting its resilience and ongoing significance in Chicano communities in the U.S. Southwest.

While significant scholarship exists on curanderismo, opportunities remain to build a more holistic understanding of its practices and significance. Much of the current work centers on Mexican or U.S.-based contexts, leaving the vibrant traditions of Central and South America, such as those in Guatemala or the Andes, underexplored. This book moves beyond filling gaps in scholarship by taking a holistic, multidisciplinary approach that is freed from the constraints commonly found in academic publishing. It embodies its subject not just in content but also in form—curanderismo as a way of being, relating, and knowing. By amplifying the voices of contemporary curanderas innovating in urban, diasporic, and digital spaces, it honors their adaptations to modern challenges. It also explores intersections with queer identity, the role of curanderismo in addressing environmental crises, and its potential integration with modern health-care systems. This work weaves together these diverse threads into a relational, transformative narrative that reflects the dynamic and evolving spirit of curanderismo itself.

This book builds on the foundations laid by previous scholarship while addressing the gaps left by it, offering new perspectives and contributions. It expands the geographic scope by including practices from the Andes, Guatemala, and other regions of Central and South America, grounding curanderismo in its broader Latin American context. By exploring the voices of modern curanderas innovating in urban and digital spaces, it highlights how the tradition continues to thrive in contemporary settings. This book also reclaims the role of queer and gender-expansive healers within curanderismo, offering a framework that embraces intersectionality and inclusivity. Furthermore, it situates curanderismo in relation to global ecological challenges, underscoring its relevance as a practice of environmental resilience and resistance. Drawing from interviews and oral histories, this book centers the voices of living practitioners, weaving their stories into an analysis that honors the tradition's past while envisioning its future. Through these contributions, this book not only honors the legacy of curanderismo but also reimagines its potential as a practice of healing, resistance, and transformation in the modern world.

This book is a journey through the history and spirit of curanderas, weaving together the past and the present, the archival and the poetic, the personal and the communal. Each chapter begins with a foundation of history, drawing from archival records, oral histories, and community knowledge. From this foundation rises the voice of the curandera herself, through stories and poems that bring her world to life.

Chapter 1, "Madre Tierra Speaks," explores the Indigenous roots of curanderismo, tracing its origins in sacred connections to the land, plants, and cosmology. It delves into how curanderas drew their knowledge from the earth itself, understanding the spiritual and physical properties of plants in order to create remedies that healed not only the body but also the spirit.

Chapter 2, "Brujas or Santas," focuses on colonial disruption and adaptation, while carefully examining how curanderas survived persecution during colonization. By blending Indigenous knowledge with Catholic traditions, curanderas preserved their healing practices through innovation and resilience, resisting erasure and reclaiming their place as healers.

Chapter 3, "Healing Fronteras," tells the stories of curanderas working in circumstances of migration and diaspora, healing the wounds of displacement and survival in the borderlands. Curanderas serve as cultural anchors and spiritual guides, creating spaces of healing and helping communities maintain cultural identity and resilience across geographic and spiritual borders.

Chapter 4, "Limpiando the Spirit," focuses on spiritual rituals such as limpias, altars, and prayers, examining how curanderismo reconnects the body and soul to the sacred. By performing rituals rooted in ancient cosmologies, curanderas offer holistic and transformative healing that merges the physical and the spiritual.

Chapter 5, "From Madre Tierra We Rise," looks to the modern revival of curanderismo as part of a global movement for decolonial healing. It centers on the communal dimensions of curanderismo and its relationship to the earth, the elements, and shared ancestral lifeways.

Chapter 6, "Curanderismo Across Diasporas," explores how curanderismo flourishes in new lands, embracing the diverse identities of those who carry it forward. It examines how practitioners adapt their practices to urban landscapes, incorporate local and global traditions, and address the challenges of displacement and belonging.

Chapter 7, "New-Gen Healers," highlights the ingenuity of contemporary curanderas who transform urban spaces into healing sanctuaries, cultivate medicinal gardens, and craft rituals that reflect gender expansiveness and identity fluidity. These practitioners honor curanderismo's traditions while ensuring its relevance for modern, diverse communities.

Chapter 8, "Queering Curanderismo," explores the intersection of queerness and curanderismo, reclaiming the roles of gender-diverse healers historically erased by colonial impositions. Through testimonios, rituals, and poetry, it celebrates queer practitioners who redefine healing as deeply inclusive and transformative.

Chapter 9, "Transnational Curanderismo," examines how curanderismo transcends borders, blending ancestral wisdom with contemporary global movements. It explores curanderismo's relevance in global healing practices, its role in ecological and decolonial struggles, and how it adapts to modern contexts while honoring its roots. This chapter highlights curanderismo's power to bridge cultures, communities, and generations, offering a transformative vision of healing for the world.

Each chapter offers a blend of history, storytelling, and poetry to illuminate the enduring power and relevance of curanderas. Together, these chapters reveal a legacy of healing that transcends time and space, inviting readers to reconnect with their own roots and to carry the spirit of the curandera forward. Readers are invited to walk this path—not as passive observers, but as seekers, reconnecting with the sacred in themselves and the world. This legacy of healing demands not only remembrance but action.

In an era of ecological crisis, systemic oppression, and the erasure of ancestral knowledge, curanderismo offers a path back to connection—connection to the earth, to spirit, and to each other. Its lessons are more vital than ever, teaching us how to heal not only our individual wounds but the fractures in our collective humanity.

This is not just a book; it is a prayer, a song, a summons. The curandera calls to you—not from a distant past, but from within the marrow of your own being. Her voice rises with the smoke of sacred herbs, it whispers in the rustle of leaves, it echoes in the spaces where stories are kept alive. She calls to remind you of your inheritance: the power to heal, to reclaim, to resist. This journey is not for the passive observer. It is for the seeker, the one willing to dig their hands into the soil of history and unearth the truths buried there. It is for those ready to mend the fractures inflicted by colonization, to restore what was stolen from the earth, from our spirits, and from our communities. The curandera's wisdom is not a relic of the past; it is a fire still burning, waiting to ignite the hearts of those who listen.

Ask yourself: Where do you turn for healing? What stories have you inherited that you carry in your blood, whether spoken aloud or whispered in dreams? The curandera's call is not for passive listening; it is a call to action, a challenge to remember and reclaim. Healing is not just the work of the curandera; it is your work too. With every step you take on this path, you contribute to a world where balance can be restored, where history can be rewritten, and where the earth's voice is heard again.

You are invited to walk this path—not as an outsider, but as someone called to remember. Remember the stories carried in your blood, the prayers whispered for you before you were born, and the resilience of those who came before you. The curandera reminds you that healing is not only about the body; it is about the soul, the land, and the collective spirit that binds us all. This is not just a book; it is a fire lit in the shadows, a voice rising from the earth itself. The curandera calls you to remember your connection to the land, to spirit, and to each other. She reminds you that every act of healing—of listening, of reclaiming, of resisting—is a thread in the consciousness of our collective survival. The path awaits. Step into the circle. Answer the call.

This legacy of healing is deeply rooted in the land itself—a sacred teacher and a source of resilience for countless generations. The story of curanderismo begins with the profound relationship between Indigenous communities and Madre Tierra, whose knowledge shaped their understanding of healing as a holistic practice. Open these pages, and let her guide you. Let her teach you to see the sacred in the ordinary, to feel the earth's pulse beneath your feet, and to understand that every act of healing is an act of revolution. The curandera is waiting. The world is waiting. It is time.

CHAPTER 1

MADRE TIERRA SPEAKS

OPENING INVOCATION

Te llamo desde las entrañas de la tierra,
desde los volcanes que guardan el fuego,
desde las raíces que gritan bajo el peso de los siglos.

I am the breath of the cornfields,
the pulse of rivers winding through stone,
the memory of flowers crushed beneath conquest.

Every leaf carries a secret; every shadow, a prayer.
The soil remembers everything.
The hands that plant, the feet that flee, the tears that fall like rain.

Te llamo, hija de los vientos, hijo del sol,
porque tu sangre lleva la canción de los jaguares,
y tus huesos son el polvo de las estrellas.
I call to you, child of the winds, child of the sun,
for your blood carries the song of jaguars,
and your bones are the dust of stars.

Escucha las montañas; ellas murmuran tu nombre.
Escucha los ríos; ellos cuentan tus historias.
Listen to the mountains; they murmur your name.
Listen to the rivers; they tell your stories.

Mira el maíz; su tallo se curva hacia el cielo.
Mira las piedras; ellas guardan la memoria de nuestros pasos.
Look at the corn; its stalk bends toward the sky.
Look at the stones; they carry the memory of our steps.

Con mis manos recojo las historias de mis ancestros.
With my hands, I gather the stories of my ancestors.
Con mi voz despierto la memoria dormida en la tierra.
With my voice, I awaken the memory sleeping in the earth.

Camina conmigo.
Let the mountains teach you strength.
Let the rivers teach you patience.
Let the earth remind you that healing begins where we have been broken.

Somos los hijos de la tierra, los nietos del sol.
We are the children of the earth, the grandchildren of the sun.
Por cada cicatriz en su piel, ella florece de nuevo.
For every scar on her skin, she blooms again.

Madre Tierra, guíanos.
Earth Mother, guide us.
Enséñanos a sanar como tú sanas:
con raíces profundas, con hojas que abrazan la luz,
con la fuerza de quienes nunca se rinden.
Teach us to heal as you heal:
with deep roots, with leaves that embrace the light,
with the strength of those who never surrender.

Te llamo, porque somos uno contigo.
I call to you, because we are one with you.
Somos los que caminan entre tus sombras,

los que cantan con tu viento,
los que recuerdan.
We are the ones who walk in your shadows,
the ones who sing with your wind,
the ones who remember.

Let the earth remind you that healing begins where we have been broken.

PRECOLONIAL FOUNDATIONS

In the time before the world was divided by borders, before the land was marked by lines that bled, the earth was revered as sacred. Tlalli, the Nahuatl name for the earth, was not simply soil; she was a mother. Her body fed the people, clothed them, healed them, and carried their stories. In the Andes, she was Pachamama, whose breath moved through the mountains and whose tears nourished the valleys. Across these lands, the earth was alive, a force as powerful as the sun or the stars.

The curanderas of these times were not healers of flesh alone; they were keepers of balance. Among the Nahua, the ticitl—the wise ones—walked between worlds. Their remedies were drawn from the land, their prayers carried on the wind. They knew that sickness was never isolated; it was the body mourning its disconnection from the spirit, the land, or the community.

Their tools were as much spiritual as they were physical. The Codex Badianus, an early colonial document that attempted to codify Indigenous knowledge, lists plants like cacao and copal, describing their medicinal uses. But this text, although written in Nahuatl by Indigenous scholars, was interpreted through the eyes of conquerors and could never capture the reverence with which each plant was harvested. A curandera did not simply pluck a leaf or cut a root. She spoke to the plant, asked permission, and gave thanks. Her hands moved with ritual precision, as though each action was a prayer.

Above her, the stars served as guides. To the Maya, the movements of the heavens were intertwined with the cycles of life. The curandera's work was often timed to the rhythms of the cosmos, aligning her rituals with the turning of the seasons and the phases of the moon. For her, the universe was a living being, and she was its humble caretaker.

This was healing as it was meant to be—holistic, sacred, and deeply connected to the rhythms of the earth and sky. It was not medicine for profit or power; it was medicine for survival, for harmony, for remembering who we are.

But the earth was more than a source of remedies or guidance—it was a teacher, offering lessons in resilience, patience, and balance. For curanderas, the land was not just a place to heal; it was a sacred partner, alive with wisdom that extended beyond the boundaries of the physical world.

Among the Nahua people, the healers known as ticitl viewed illness as a disruption in the balance between the body, spirit, and earth. Their remedies often included ritual offerings to the land and sky, emphasizing the interconnectedness of all life. For example, cacao beans were not merely ground into medicinal drinks but imbued with prayers to the gods of rain and fertility, ensuring harmony between human needs and natural cycles. These ceremonies reflected a worldview in which healing the individual also meant honoring the earth's sacred rhythms.

THE LAND AS SACRED TEACHER

The land is not silent. It breathes through the wind that bends the trees, it hums through the roots that thread the soil, and it speaks in the language of leaves and stones. To the curandera, the earth is more than a provider; it is a teacher, a guide, and an elder whose wisdom is both ancient and eternal.

In Indigenous cosmologies, every plant carries a spirit, and every spirit has a purpose. To gather a healing herb is not an act of ownership but an exchange. The curandera kneels before the earth, her hands pressed to the soil as she whispers her gratitude. She asks permission, knowing that the plant she takes is a gift, not a right. In return, she offers a prayer, a song, or a handful of water poured at the base of the roots. This reciprocity is sacred, a bond of trust between healer and earth.

In the Nahua tradition, the sacred cornfields were seen as the heart of the community. The planting and harvesting of maize were rituals guided by the rhythms of the cosmos. The curandera, like the farmer, worked in harmony with these cycles, knowing that her remedies would fail if the land was mistreated. In the Andes, the coca plant was considered a bridge between the physical and spiritual worlds. It was chewed to give strength, brewed to heal illness, and offered to the mountains in ceremonies of gratitude. In both traditions, the land was not merely a source of medicine; it was the medicine.

The earth teaches patience through its seasons, resilience through its ability to heal after devastation, and generosity through its endless gifts. This reciprocal relationship extended to agricultural practices as well. For instance, Andean farmers aligned their planting with lunar cycles, believing that the moon's energy guided the earth's fertility. Curanderas not only gave advice on these practices but also served as spiritual intermediaries, leading ceremonies to bless seeds before planting and thanking the soil during harvest. These rituals, steeped in gratitude, ensured that the land was treated not as a resource to exploit but as a living partner in survival.

The curandera learns to listen, to observe the signs that the land provides. A sudden bloom of wildflowers may signal a change in the air; the behavior of animals may foretell a shift in the weather. Every detail is a lesson, every moment an opportunity to deepen her connection to the world around her.

Yet this relationship is not without its demands. The land expects care in return for its gifts. The curandera must tend the soil, water the plants, and protect the fragile ecosystems that sustain her work. She understands that to harm the earth is to harm herself and her community. The teachings of the land are clear: healing is not an individual act but a collective responsibility.

Yet this relationship, so integral to the balance of life, has faced profound disruption. When the colonizers arrived, they saw the land not as sacred but as something to dominate. Harmony was shattered by the arrival of colonizers, whose worldview turned the sacred into something to exploit. Where the curandera saw the earth as a partner, the colonizers saw it as a commodity. This rupture would mark the beginning of a profound and violent disruption. The curandera, who lived in harmony with the earth, became a symbol of resistance in a world that sought to erase her knowledge and sever her connection to the land.

COLONIAL DISRUPTION: THE FRACTURE OF EARTH AND SPIRIT

In what is now Mexico, the Nahua people revered the earth as Tlalli, a living entity that nourished and sustained all life. To the Spanish, however, the land was soil to be claimed, tilled, and mined. Across the Andes, where the Quechua people of present-day Peru and Bolivia honored Pachamama as the mother of all creation, the colonizers imposed a starkly different view: the earth was property, its value measured in gold and crops. This shift was not merely physical—it was spiritual. The colonizers sought to sever the profound connection between Indigenous peoples and the earth, knowing that to break this bond was to weaken the communities that thrived upon it.

Curanderas, who embodied this connection to the land and its sacred wisdom, became prime targets of colonial systems. The Catholic Church, in its efforts to dismantle Indigenous belief systems, labeled their practices witchcraft or heresy. Rituals once performed openly, calling upon the spirits of the earth and cosmos, were demonized and forced into secrecy. For example, a record from the Archivo General de la Nación in Mexico details the case of María, a Nahua healer from present-day central Mexico, who was tried in 1612 for engaging in "superstitious" practices. María used herbal remedies and whispered prayers to treat a neighbor's fever, acts described by her accusers as both "miraculous" and "dangerous." Her trial reflects a broader pattern: the colonizers feared the power of curanderas while quietly relying on their knowledge.

Colonial records also document instances in which Indigenous knowledge was appropriated. The sixteenth-century encyclopedic botanical manuscript known as the Codex Badianus attempted to catalog the medicinal practices of Indigenous healers while stripping them of their spiritual significance. This text, while celebrated as an early medical guide, reflects the colonizers' paradoxical reliance on and dismissal of curanderismo. By recording remedies while dismissing the curandera's rituals as "superstition," colonizers sought to claim her knowledge while erasing her authority.

Similar patterns of suppression and adaptation occurred elsewhere. The Quechua people of the Andes, whose healers used coca leaves in rituals to honor the mountains and alleviate sickness, saw these sacred practices condemned as diabolical. Yet colonial administrators depended on coca's medicinal and energizing properties, even incorporating it into European-style remedies. Records from the Archivo General de Indias in Seville describe coca's widespread use in Andean rituals, noting with unease its spiritual significance.

In what is now Chile, the Mapuche people relied on machi, spiritual healers who acted as intermediaries between the physical and spiritual worlds. These healers used plants like canelo, a sacred tree believed to hold protective powers, in their rituals. Spanish records describe the machi as both feared and revered, with colonial officials documenting their ceremonies in detail, often for the purpose of suppression. Despite these efforts, the machi continued their work, blending their knowledge with elements of Catholicism to protect their traditions and communities.

Colonization also attempted to erase the languages that carried these traditions. Nahuatl terms like *yauhtli*, the name of a plant used by the Nahua for spiritual cleansing in what is now Mexico, were replaced with Spanish names like *tagetes*. The Codex Badianus translates these sacred plants into clinical descriptions, stripping away their spiritual significance. In the Andes, the Quechua names for sacred herbs like muña were similarly replaced in colonial texts, rendering the plants commodities rather than sacred beings.

The disruption extended to sacred spaces. In Mexico, the hill of Tepeyac, a site revered by the Nahua as the dwelling of Tonantzin, the earth mother, was transformed into a shrine for the Virgin of Guadalupe. This act of appropriation reflected a broader colonial strategy: overlay Indigenous cosmologies with Catholic symbols, replacing but not entirely erasing them. This syncretism, while forced, also became a tool of resistance. Curanderas wove Indigenous prayers into Catholic hymns, continued their rituals under the guise of saintly devotions, and transformed altars into spaces where Tonantzin and the Virgin Mary became one.

Despite the violence of colonization, the relationship between curanderas and the earth endured. Oral traditions flourished in secrecy, passing knowledge from generation to generation. Mothers whispered to daughters about the plants that cured fevers, the prayers that called for rain, and the rituals that protected the spirit. These stories ensured that the curandera's wisdom survived, even as the colonial world sought to bury it.

Among the K'iche' Maya of present-day Guatemala, the ajq'ijab, or daykeepers, upheld their sacred traditions by working with the Cholq'ij, a spiritual calendar central to their cosmology. Through carefully performed rituals, they balanced the spiritual energies of individuals and communities, using incense, candles, and sacred altars to preserve harmony and well-being. Colonial authorities sought to outlaw these ceremonies, describing them as "idolatrous" in court records now preserved in the Archivo General de Centro América—a term often used to imply devil worship or practices deemed heretical by colonial religious standards. However, oral traditions ensured the survival of these practices, with knowledge passed down through families despite the risks of persecution.

The land, too, bore witness. The mountains of Peru sheltered rituals in their folds, far from the eyes of colonizers. The forests of Mesoamerica shielded healers as they gathered herbs for remedies. In the face of conquest, the earth remained a partner in resistance, its rivers carrying whispers of rebellion, its winds carrying prayers.

Through all of this, the curandera endured. She became a bridge between worlds, holding on to the sacred while navigating the demands of survival. Her work was an act of defiance, a quiet revolution rooted in the soil, the spirit, and the resilience of her people. In the whispers of prayers and the scent of burning copal, the curandera's wisdom survives. Even now, in urban neighborhoods and rural pueblos, her work continues—a living testament to the resilience of ancestral knowledge.

A DAY IN THE LIFE OF A PRECOLONIAL CURANDERA: THE TESTIMONIO OF IZTLI

The sun had not yet risen over the highlands of what is now central Mexico, but Iztli, a Nahua curandera, was already awake. The earth beneath her feet was cool and damp as she stepped outside, the faint scent of dew mixing with the smoky remnants of last night's fire. Around her, the maize fields stretched into the dawn, their tall stalks rustling like whispered prayers. She sought cempasúchil, the vibrant marigold whose bright petals were believed to guide spirits and heal the grieving. Known as the flower of the dead, cempasúchil would play a crucial role in the altar she planned to build later that day. Its scent was said to awaken the memories of those who had passed, bridging the worlds of the living and the departed.

Iztli walked to the edge of the field, her woven basket in hand. Today she needed epazote and yauhtli—plants whose spirits she called upon for cleansing and protection. She knelt before the first plant, her fingers brushing its delicate leaves. "Tlasojkamati," she murmured, her voice low with reverence. "Thank you for your offering." From a small pouch at her waist, she sprinkled a pinch of cacao powder at the base of the plant, a gift of gratitude to the earth.

As the first light of the sun crept over the hills, Iztli returned to her home, a modest structure built of adobe and thatched palm. Inside, a young boy and his mother awaited her. The boy's face was pale, his breathing was shallow, and his eyes fluttered with fevered dreams. The mother's hands trembled as she held him close. "Curandera," she said, her voice breaking, "he has not eaten in two days. I am afraid he will not wake."

Iztli placed her hands on the boy's forehead, feeling the heat radiating from his skin. She closed her eyes and whispered a prayer, calling upon Tonantzin, the earth mother, to lend her strength. "This is not just illness," she said softly. "His spirit is burdened."

She took a small bowl of agua de flores, infused with petals of cempasúchil and roses, and sprinkled it over the boy's chest as she murmured prayers. The fragrance filled the room, carrying her words al viento, to the ears of the earth mother. Each step of the ritual was precise, her hands guided by the teachings of her ancestors.

She moved to her altar, a sacred space adorned with clay bowls, feathers, and bundles of dried herbs. From one bowl, she took copal and placed it in a clay censer. As the smoke began to rise, she waved it over the boy's body, allowing the sacred fragrance to purify the air. She reached for the yauhtli leaves she had gathered earlier, crushing them gently in her hands to release their scent. "The plant carries its own prayers," she explained to the mother. "It will help lift what weighs him down."

Using the crushed leaves, Iztli prepared a poultice, mixing them with a few drops of water and the ashes of the copal. She placed the mixture on the boy's chest, wrapping it with a woven cloth. She then took an egg, holding it above the boy as she moved it in slow, deliberate circles from his head to his feet. All the while, she sang a song—an ancient melody passed down from her grandmother. Her voice was steady, carrying the strength of generations.

The boy's breathing began to slow, his chest rising and falling with ease. His mother gasped as his eyes fluttered open, the fever seemingly broken. Iztli placed a hand on the mother's shoulder. "Keep him close to the fire tonight," she instructed. "Boil this epazote in water and let him sip it slowly. And give thanks to the land, for it is she who has healed him."

As the mother and child left, Iztli sat quietly before her altar. She sprinkled a handful of maize kernels into the censer, an offering to Tonantzin for her guidance. Outside, the sun climbed higher into the sky, and the village stirred to life. Iztli's day was far from over. There were herbs to gather, remedies to prepare, and spirits to tend. But for now, she allowed herself a moment of stillness, listening to the hum of the earth beneath her feet.

MADRE TIERRA'S PROMISE

Tú eres de la tierra,
nacida de raíces que rompen el concreto,
de polvo y lluvia, de sangre y sol.
Your breath carries her storms,
your veins hold her rivers,
your bones are las montañas que nunca se doblan.

When they came con espadas y cruces,
cuando arrancaron los árboles y quemaron los campos,
la tierra no se rindió.
Her cenizas became semillas,
her lágrimas became oceans,
and her voice—soft but fierce—called to those who still listened.

The curandera escucha.
She walks en los caminos de piedra y sombra,
con sus manos llenas de historias,

con sus ojos llenos de memoria.
She gathers ruda to calm the spirit,
yerba santa to cleanse the soul,
copal to carry her prayers al viento.
She picks what grows donde nadie mira,
weaving remedies from what was left behind.

Her altar is simple:
a bowl of agua de flores,
a stone blessed by the river,
un ramo de romero tied with red thread.
Each piece, un puente—a bridge
between this world and the next.

This is the revolución.
Not with armas but with prayers,
not with bullets but with semillas.
Healing is rebellion.
Remembering is resistencia.
Every plant we gather, every altar we build,
every prayer we whisper
is a fight to take back what was stolen.

Madre Tierra no se olvida.
Her rivers still run,
her mountains still stand,
her winds still carry the songs of nuestras abuelas.
She waits for us,
her voice in the thunder,
her promise in the rain:

Aquí estoy.
Todavía estoy aquí.
Y tú también.

• • •

The curandera's voice echoes through these lines, reminding us that healing is not just personal—it is collective, ancestral, and revolutionary. This poem is a creative interpretation inspired by the voices and teachings of curanderas across generations, drawing from historical research, oral traditions, and works such as Edward Anthony Polanco's *Healing Like Our Ancestors: The Nahua Tiçitl, Gender, and Settler Colonialism in Central Mexico, 1535–1660*. Each stanza carries the weight of memory, the fire of resistance, and the hope of reclamation. It speaks to the enduring strength of Indigenous traditions, defying the erasures of colonization and reconnecting us to the roots that nourish our spirits. In every prayer whispered to the wind and every seed planted in defiance, Madre Tierra reminds us that she has never left us—and that we, too, are part of her unbroken promise.

While these Indigenous traditions provided the foundation for curanderismo, the arrival of colonization disrupted, suppressed, and yet ultimately transformed these practices. Curanderas, faced with the violence of cultural erasure, adapted by weaving Indigenous knowledge together with Catholic iconography and rituals, ensuring the survival of their sacred traditions. Chapter 2 explores this era of resilience, when curanderismo became both a sacred and a subversive practice of survival.

CHAPTER 2

BRUJAS OR SANTAS

OPENING INVOCATION

Somos las que sobreviven.
Nos escondemos entre sombras y fuego,
donde los vientos susurran historias que otros temen escuchar.
They call us brujas, but we are healers;
they accuse us, but we are guides.

Nos llamaron peligrosas porque conocíamos el lenguaje de la tierra,
because we spoke to the rivers and called to the stars.
Con nuestras manos recogemos la memoria,
con nuestras voces tejemos la resistencia.
We carried the songs of our abuelas,
hidden in the folds of our rebozos,
waiting for the day when they could be sung aloud.

They burned our sisters,
but they could not destroy the fire within us.
Every flame they lit became a spark,
a whisper carried on the wind,

igniting the hearts of those who listened.
Madre Tierra sigue hablando.
Her voice rises with the smoke of copal,
carried through altars hidden in plain sight.

We walk between worlds,
where prayers disguised as hymns protect our truths.
Where ruda cleanses the spirit,
and yerba santa binds the wounds colonization inflicted.
We are bridges, not witches;
santas, not heretics.
Our hands hold remedies, not curses;
our hearts hold prayers, not secrets.

Mira nuestras manos.
They carry the weight of centuries,
the knowledge of plants that heal
and spirits that guide.
They move with precision, with purpose,
drawing strength from Tonantzin,
from Pachamama,
from every madre who has ever prayed for her children.

From the Nahua prayers to Tlazolteotl,
goddess of purification,
to the Andean offerings to Pachamama,
the curandera's lineage is a constellation of sacred connections.
Each ritual is a thread in a vast tapestry woven over millennia,
a quiet rebellion against the erasure of the sacred.

These prayers are not whispers of the past;
they are seeds carried forward,
taking root in every ceremony,
every whispered limpia,
every altar built in the face of destruction.

Escucha nuestras voces.
They are the echoes of ceremonies once forbidden,
where limpias became blessings
and altars became homes.
They carry the names of the mountains,
the rivers, and the stars
that have always been our sanctuary.

We are not afraid of their labels.
Bruja is not an insult;
it is a reminder of our power.
Santa is not a pedestal;
it is a recognition of our grace.
We walk between these names,
shaping them into shields,
turning them into songs.

Con nuestras limpias, limpiamos siglos de olvido.
With our altars, we build bridges between the seen and unseen.
With our prayers, we reclaim what was taken,
piece by piece, breath by breath.
Every ritual is an act of rebellion;
every healing, an act of survival.

They fear us because we remember.
We remember the earth before their borders,
the stars before their maps,
the voices before their silence.
And in that memory lies the power to heal,
to resist, and to rebuild.

Madre Tierra still speaks.
Her rivers carry the stories of our ancestors,
her winds carry the prayers of our children.
And we are still listening.

THE DUALITY OF BRUJAS Y SANTAS

Colonization did not just take lives and the land; it sought to reframe identities. For curanderas, this meant walking a delicate line between fear and reverence, condemnation and necessity. They became symbols of duality: brujas y santas, witches and saints. The colonizers' labels often depended on context: in moments of desperation, the curandera was a healer, a protector, even a miracle worker. But when her power threatened the established order, she was a heretic, a danger, a bruja.

This binary was not a reflection of who the curandera was—it was a projection of colonial anxieties. To the colonizers, she embodied resistance, survival, and a knowledge they could not control. Yet to the communities she served, she was a lifeline, a bridge to the sacred, a defender of cultural memory.

Doña Esperanza, a contemporary curandera in Oaxaca, reflects on this legacy: "Every limpia I perform carries the prayers of those before me. Our hands remember what the world tried to erase." Her work illustrates how curanderismo continues to thrive as a living memory, in which each ritual becomes an act of cultural reclamation and resistance.

The syncretic practices of curanderas blurred these lines further. By integrating Catholic prayers and symbols into their rituals, they were both protecting their traditions and challenging colonial attempts to erase them. Their ability to navigate duality was not a sign of conflict, but of strength. This duality was embodied in the colonial imagery of the Virgin of Guadalupe. While colonizers promoted her as a Christian symbol, Indigenous communities saw her as a continuation of Tonantzin, the Nahua earth mother. For curanderas, this duality became a shield and a tool, allowing them to conduct rituals that honored Indigenous deities under the guise of Catholic devotion. The blending of the Virgin and Tonantzin was not assimilation but a quiet assertion that the sacred could adapt without surrendering its roots. It allowed curanderas to carry the sacred forward, even under the weight of colonization.

PERSECUTION AND ADAPTATION

The Spanish Inquisition was one of the curandera's greatest adversaries. Across Latin America, women accused of practicing "superstitious rites" often faced trials that sought to dismantle their power. The Archivo General de la Nación (Mexico) holds countless cases detailing such accusations. These include the 1612 record describing the Nahua healer María, mentioned above, who was accused of invoking pagan spirits and using "illicit" herbs to cure illness.

In 1655, Ana de la Cruz, a renowned curandera in Lima, faced charges of heresy for performing rituals that incorporated Andean practices like coca leaf readings. The transcripts of her trial reveal her defense: "I heal by the grace of God, as my grandmothers before me did." By invoking both Catholic faith and ancestral lineage, Ana embodied the hybridity of curanderismo during colonization, preserving her community's traditions while navigating colonial power structures. This persecution of curanderas like Ana de la Cruz was not uncommon during the colonial period, as Indigenous and African-descended healers frequently faced accusations of heresy or witchcraft for engaging in practices rooted in ancestral traditions. Anderson Hagler's dissertation "Excesses of Religion: Indigenous and African Descent Peoples, Catholicism, and the Management of the Supernatural in Colonial Mexico" highlights how colonial authorities sought to regulate and suppress these practices, viewing them as challenges to Catholic orthodoxy. Yet, as Hagler notes, practitioners often blended Catholic and Indigenous spiritual frameworks to protect their communities and resist cultural erasure. Ana's defense, invoking both her grandmothers and divine grace, exemplifies this syncretism, illustrating how curanderismo adapted to survive amid the constraints of colonial power.

The persecution of curanderas often mirrored broader colonial anxieties about Indigenous autonomy. By labeling them brujas or witches, colonial authorities sought to delegitimize their spiritual and communal roles. However, records reveal that even as priests condemned curanderas, they often relied on their remedies for fevers, childbirth complications, and agricultural plagues. This contradiction underscores the curandera's enduring role as a healer, even in a world that sought to erase her.

This contradiction was common. In Peru, Quechua healers who used coca leaves in rituals to honor the apus—mountain spirits—were branded as diabolical. Yet colonial officials themselves used coca to treat altitude sickness and fatigue. In Guatemala, K'iche' Maya daykeepers were condemned for maintaining ancestral altars, even as their spiritual knowledge was quietly preserved within families.

To survive, curanderas adapted. They wove Catholic prayers into their rituals, replacing the names of Indigenous deities with those of saints. In Mexico, rituals to honor Tonantzin were conducted under the guise of devotions to the Virgin of Guadalupe. In the Andes, healers continued to make offerings to Pachamama while invoking Catholic saints. These adaptations were not signs of assimilation—they were acts of defiance, ensuring the survival of curanderismo.

THE ROLE OF SYNCRETISM

Syncretism was both a shield and a weapon. By blending Catholicism with Indigenous traditions, curanderas protected their practices from colonial scrutiny while creating a powerful spiritual synthesis. This fusion allowed them to reframe rituals as acts of faith while maintaining their sacred essence.

In rural Oaxaca, for instance, curanderas incorporated Catholic saints into their altars, pairing images of Saint Francis with offerings of maize and cacao. These altars became bridges between two worlds, where prayers to saints often echoed precolonial invocations. The use of ruda in cleansing rituals, framed as a blessing from God, masked its ancient role as a plant of protection and purification. Rituals involving maize, sacred waters, and healing herbs were central to curanderas' survival during colonial times. By performing offerings to Pachamama or Tlazolteotl, these healers maintained spiritual ties to the land while integrating elements of Catholic practice. For instance, offerings of corn mixed with holy water became common, symbolizing the merging of ancestral and imposed traditions. Today, these rituals resonate with ecofeminist movements, emphasizing the interconnected healing of body and earth. Through these adaptations, curanderas preserved not only their practices but also the spiritual significance that colonization sought to erase.

Limpias (cleansings): Curanderas performed limpias under the guise of blessings, invoking saints like San Rafael while secretly calling upon the earth's energies. The egg often used in limpias was said to absorb negative energy and restore balance—a practice that aligned with both Indigenous cosmology and Catholic symbolism.

Altars: The altars of curanderas became spaces of resistance. While they prominently featured Catholic icons, these images often served as placeholders for Indigenous deities. A figure of the Virgin Mary might be paired with offerings of maize and cacao, tying Catholic imagery to Indigenous spirituality.

Herbal remedies: Plants like ruda and epazote, sacred in Indigenous healing, were reframed in Christian terms. Their powers were attributed to divine creation, masking their deeper connections to precolonial traditions.

This syncretism was not an erasure but a reimagining. By integrating Catholic elements, curanderas ensured that their practices could persist in a colonial world. Yet beneath these adaptations lay the unbroken threads of their ancestral knowledge.

One notable example of syncretism is the transformation of the Danza de los Voladores, a Mesoamerican ritual honoring the rain gods, into a "festival dance" sanctioned by colonial authorities. Similarly, in the Andes, offerings to Pachamama were disguised as blessings to the Virgin Mary, with coca leaves and maize presented as "harvest gifts." These acts were not concessions but strategies, preserving the sacred under layers of colonial oversight.

THE FEAR OF THE BRUJA

The fear of the curandera—labeled as bruja—was deeply rooted in colonial efforts to control both bodies and spirits. To the colonizers, her knowledge of plants, her connection to the earth, and her role as a spiritual guide made her dangerous. She held power outside the colonial framework, and that power threatened the systems of control that sought to dominate every aspect of Indigenous life.

The label of bruja was a weapon of the colonizer. It dehumanized the curandera, framing her as a threat to the Christian order. Inquisition records often described her remedies as curses and her rituals as pacts with the devil. This fear was compounded by the curandera's ability to navigate both spiritual and physical realms. Her remedies, often rooted in an intimate knowledge of plants, were seen as unnatural or even diabolical in a colonial worldview that valued domination over understanding. Yet to her community, the curandera represented resilience. Her so-called witchcraft was not a rejection of Christianity but a testament to the enduring power of ancestral knowledge—a power that colonial authorities could neither fully suppress nor comprehend. The same Inquisition records also reveal an undeniable reliance on her work. Priests and colonial officials frequently sought out curanderas for healing, even as they condemned them.

To the communities she served, however, the curandera was never just a healer—she was a protector, a bridge between the physical and spiritual realms. Her "witchcraft" was nothing more than the survival of knowledge that colonization could not erase.

The label of bruja was more than a slur—it was a colonial strategy to undermine Indigenous autonomy. By framing curanderas as witches, the colonizers sought to delegitimize their roles as spiritual leaders and healers. This fear extended beyond the individual: it was a fear of collective resistance. To call a curandera a bruja was to attack the knowledge she carried, the community she protected, and the spiritual networks she upheld.

A MIDNIGHT RITUAL: TESTIMONIO OF XOCHITL

The family arrived in secret.

The knock at Xochitl's door was soft but insistent, a sound that carried fear as much as desperation. A man stepped into the dimly lit room, his face shadowed by the brim of his hat. Behind him, a woman clutched a bundle to her chest—a child, his face pale and his breathing shallow.

"Please," the man whispered. "He has been sick for days. The priest would not help us. They said to pray, but . . ." His voice faltered, his hands trembling.

Xochitl nodded. "Put him here," she said, motioning to a woven mat near her altar. The altar was modest: a statue of the Virgin of Guadalupe, a small bowl of copal, and bundles of dried ruda and epazote. But beneath the altar lay a hidden offering to Tonantzin—maize kernels, cacao, and a clay figurine of the earth mother.

She began the limpia with holy water, sprinkling it over the child's body as she murmured prayers to the Virgin. But her voice carried older words, too, hidden beneath the cadence of Catholic hymns. "Tonantzin, madre de la tierra, guía mis manos," she whispered, tracing the sign of the cross over the child's forehead.

Using the ruda, she swept the air around him, drawing out the sickness she could feel lingering in his spirit. The egg, smooth and cool in her palm, moved in slow circles over his chest. The copal smoke thickened, rising in spirals toward the low ceiling, carrying her prayers into the night.

The child's breathing steadied, his small body relaxing as the ritual ended. Xochitl turned to the parents. "Boil this epazote in water," she instructed, handing them a bundle of herbs. "Let him drink it slowly, and keep him warm tonight."

They left with quiet gratitude, their shadows disappearing into the darkness. Xochitl sat alone before her altar, her hands still tingling with the energy of the ritual. The Virgin watched her in silence, but Xochitl's prayers were for Tonantzin.

As the family disappeared into the shadows, Xochitl remained kneeling before her altar. She knew that each ritual carried a risk. If the wrong eyes saw the copal smoke rising from her home or heard the Nahuatl words in her prayers, she could face the same fate as so many others—tried, punished, erased. Yet she also knew that to stop would carry a greater risk: the risk of forgetting, of letting the sacred slip away into silence. Her work was an act of defiance, rooted in the belief that healing was resistance and memory was survival.

THE BRUJA'S PRAYER

We are the daughters of the soil,
the ones they tried to burn
but could not silence.

Nos llamaron brujas,
pero somos guardianas.
They called us witches,
but we are the keepers of memory,
the voices of rivers and roots.

Our prayers rise like smoke—
soft, persistent, unbroken.
We whisper to the earth,
to the stars, to the spirits
who walked these lands before borders bled them.

Madre Tierra, they fear us because we remember.
We remember the songs of our abuelas,
the names of the plants that heal,
the words that summon rain.
They fear us because we walk between worlds,
because we see what they want us to forget.

Their crosses could not bind us.
Their trials could not break us.
In the flames, we became the fire,
carrying the light of resistance
into every shadowed corner.

Con nuestras manos sanamos,
con nuestras voces luchamos,
con nuestras almas resistimos.
With our hands, we heal.
With our voices, we fight.
With our spirits, we resist.

They call us brujas, but we are something more.
We are bridges to the sacred,
builders of altars hidden in plain sight.
We are the prayers whispered into the wind,
the fire that survives.

Madre Tierra, tú sigues hablando.
And we are still listening.

• • •

The curandera's power lies not only in her remedies but in her refusal to vanish. She stands as a reminder that healing is political, that survival is resistance, and that every prayer whispered into the wind is a call to action. Her legacy is carried in the hands of every healer, in the voices of every storyteller, and in the hearts of those who dare to remember.

The legacy of colonization not only shaped the practices of curanderas but also created new landscapes of displacement and migration. Borders, both physical and spiritual, became spaces of survival and healing as communities sought to reclaim their identities and traditions. Chapter 3 examines these borderlands as powerful spaces of resistance, where curanderas continue their work as healers and cultural anchors.

CHAPTER 3

HEALING FRONTERAS

OPENING INVOCATION

Te llamo desde las fronteras,
desde las líneas que cortan la tierra y las almas.
I call to you from the borders,
from the lines that cut the land and the soul.

Donde la tierra se parte, el espíritu se fortalece.
Where the earth splits, the spirit grows stronger.
Donde los caminos se cruzan, nacen nuevas historias.
Where the paths cross, new stories are born.

Somos las que caminan con el polvo en los pies,
con la luna como guía, con el sol como esperanza.
We are those who walk with dust on our feet,
the moon as our guide, the sun as our hope.

Cargamos la memoria de nuestros ancestros,
como rebozos llenos de sueños y cicatrices.
We carry the memory of our ancestors,
like shawls filled with dreams and scars.

Con nuestras manos, tejemos puentes.
Con nuestras voces, sanamos heridas.
With our hands, we weave bridges.
With our voices, we heal wounds.

Somos las semillas que cruzan el viento,
que brotan en tierras desconocidas,
que encuentran raíces donde nadie las espera.
We are the seeds carried by the wind,
sprouting in unfamiliar lands,
finding roots where none expect them.

Te llamo, porque las fronteras no nos definen.
I call to you, because borders do not define us.
Somos más grandes que las líneas que nos dividen.
We are greater than the lines that divide us.

Las fronteras respiran,
y en su aliento encontramos sanación.
The borders breathe,
and in their breath, we find healing.

Somos las que cruzan con raíces en el alma,
con hojas de ocotillo como escudo y el río como frontera sagrada.
We are those who cross with roots in our souls,
with ocotillo leaves as our shield and the river as a sacred border.

• • •

This invocation draws inspiration from Gloria Anzaldúa's concept of the border as an open wound—both a site of pain and a place of transformation. Anzaldúa frames the border as a place where division and connection coexist, birthing new identities and stories through what she calls the *mestiza consciousness*. In this invocation, the border becomes more than a wound; it is imagined as a site of healing, a place where curanderas weave bridges and mend the displacements caused by colonization, migration, and systemic oppression.

Building upon Anzaldúa's framework, this chapter introduces the curandera as a healer of displacement—someone who tends to the spiritual, cultural, and physical wounds inflicted by fractured geographies and histories. Where Anzaldúa highlights the liminal space of the border as a site of creative resistance, this work extends her vision by exploring how curanderas embody and enact that healing process. They transform the border from a place of division to one of sanctuary and connection, using rituals, plants, and ancestral wisdom to help individuals and communities reclaim their sense of belonging. In this way, the curandera's work is an act of defiance and reclamation, challenging the forces of erasure while creating spaces where healing and resilience flourish. This chapter weaves their voices and practices into the broader narrative of sanación—collective healing that transcends boundaries, both literal and metaphorical.

THE CURANDERA AS A HEALER OF DISPLACEMENT

In the dusty streets of border towns, amid the chaos of migration and exile, curanderas have long served as anchors for the displaced. These healers tend to the physical and emotional wounds of those who cross lands that are not their own, offering remedies and rituals that reconnect them to their roots.

Migrants often arrive with bodies broken by the journey and spirits heavy with grief. A limp sustained on rocky terrain, the relentless fatigue of walking for days without rest, or the silent trauma of leaving a homeland behind—all of these demand the touch of a curandera. Her remedies are born from the land itself: yerba buena for digestion troubled by unfamiliar food, valeriana to calm restless nerves, and copal to cleanse the spirit weighed down by fear.

During the Mexican Revolution, families fleeing violence sought refuge in border towns like Ciudad Juárez and Tijuana. Oral histories recount curanderas offering remedies for the physical toll of travel—aloe vera for blistered feet and teas of manzanilla for frayed nerves. These curanderas became symbols of hope, reminding migrants that even in displacement, the land provided healing.

Yet the curandera's role extends beyond healing physical ailments. Curanderas in migration hubs also serve as cultural anchors, preserving traditions that migrants risk losing in displacement. In shelters near the Texas border, curanderas often create makeshift altars adorned with photographs, dried herbs, and candles. These sacred spaces become communal centers, where migrants pray for protection and strength. Through these rituals, the curandera not only addresses individual grief but also reinforces the collective identity of displaced communities, reminding them that their roots remain unbroken.

The curandera becomes a keeper of hope, creating altars that honor both the ancestors left behind and the future yet to be built. These altars, sacred yet often simple, include photos of loved ones, offerings of corn or beans, and candles lit for protection. In their glow, migrants find a moment of solace, a reminder that they are not alone.

Migrants walking the deserts of the Sonoran borderlands often carry herbs gifted by curanderas, such as ruda for protection and epazote to ease digestion disrupted by scarce water and harsh food. These gifts are not mere objects; they carry prayers woven into their preparation, each leaf and root imbued with the intentions of survival and resilience. Oral histories from shelters near Nogales recount how curanderas would often create talismans for children, tying red threads around their wrists as symbols of grounding and safety. These small acts of care turn the chaos of migration into moments of sacred connection, reminding migrants that the earth itself walks with them.

BORDERS AS SPACES OF HEALING AND RESISTANCE

Borders are often imagined as divisions, but for curanderas they are spaces of transformation. In these liminal spaces, where cultures meet and histories collide, the work of healing becomes both deeply personal and profoundly political.

Curanderas in borderlands serve as bridges, connecting fractured communities and preserving the sacred in the face of erasure. In the U.S.-Mexico borderlands, stories abound of curanderas who tend to migrants waiting in shelters, offering both spiritual and practical care. In these liminal spaces, curanderas weave together traditions from diverse cultures, creating a tapestry of shared resilience. For instance, in El Paso, a curandera might use yerba buena from her Mexican heritage alongside eucalyptus leaves shared by Central American migrants. This blending of practices turns the borderlands into a place of spiritual innovation, where healing rituals become acts of solidarity that transcend national and cultural boundaries.

At one shelter near Tijuana, a curandera named doña Carmen gathers women in a circle each evening, transforming the shelter's courtyard into a sacred space of healing and connection. She teaches them to weave prayers into rosaries, each bead threaded with intentions of protection and resilience. Alongside this, doña Carmen shares her knowledge of herbal medicine, showing the women how to identify plants like ruda and epazote growing along the roadside. These herbs, often overlooked by passersby, become symbols of empowerment as the women learn to prepare poultices for aches and for anxious nerves. They even assemble small sachets of protective herbs to carry on their journeys. Through her teachings, doña Carmen not only provides practical remedies but also nurtures a sense of agency and community, reminding the women that their hands carry the wisdom of countless generations. The circle becomes more than a lesson—it is a space where healing transcends the physical, affirming the women's strength and their ability to reclaim hope even in the harshest of circumstances.

In the 1930s, as deportation raids swept through Mexican American border communities under the guise of "repatriation" programs, curanderas emerged as quiet but powerful resisters. Exhibits at the Museo del Westside in San Antonio highlight the historical roles of midwives, herbalists, and healers, underscoring the cultural and spiritual significance of these practices. Additional resources, such as the collections at the Briscoe Center for American History at the University of Texas at Austin, include oral histories and personal papers documenting how curanderas in El Paso and San Diego created clandestine spaces for ritual and healing. Backyard altars, often adorned with images of the Virgin of Guadalupe, bowls of copal, and offerings of maize, served as sites of both prayer and political defiance. Oral testimonies also describe gatherings under mesquite trees at dusk, where curanderas led limpias and offered herbal remedies for physical and emotional wounds. These spaces provided more than immediate relief; they reinforced a shared cultural identity that colonial systems sought to dismantle. The act of lighting a candle or invoking ancestral spirits became a form of resistance, asserting that curanderismo traditions could not be erased. These spaces were sanctuaries not only for the body but also for the spirit, reminding displaced families that their heritage was a source of strength and survival.

These acts are not mere gestures; they are acts of resistance. By preserving the knowledge of healing traditions, curanderas challenge the colonial systems that sought to sever Indigenous people from their land, culture, and identity. At the same time, they offer tools for survival, helping migrants navigate not just the physical challenge of crossing but the spiritual fractures caused by displacement.

THE SPIRITUAL BORDERLANDS

For curanderas, borders are not just physical; they are spiritual thresholds. In these spaces, where the past and present intertwine, the curandera's work becomes a bridge between worlds. She helps migrants navigate both the journey of the body and the journey of the soul.

A curandera preparing a migrant family for their crossing might provide talismans for protection: a bundle of ruda tied with red thread, a prayer whispered over a coin to be carried in the pocket, or a small vial of agua de flores to sprinkle on the ground if fear takes hold. These items are not mere superstitions; they are symbols of connection, anchoring the migrant to a lineage that spans centuries. The spiritual power of the borderlands lies in their duality: they are places of separation but also of connection. For curanderas, crossing a border is more than a physical act—it is a spiritual journey. Through rituals like sprinkling agua de rosas on the ground before stepping into unknown territory, they invoke the protection and guidance of their ancestors. These acts remind migrants that even in unfamiliar lands, they are never truly alone; their spirits carry the wisdom of those who came before.

Milagros, tiny metal charms shaped like hearts or arms, often accompany the prayers of curanderas in the borderlands. Infused with the scent of sage and carried in woven pouches, these tokens symbolize the desires and fears of those crossing. Whether invoking Tonantzin, the Virgin of Guadalupe, or a celestial spirit, the curandera's rituals are bridges that connect the seen and unseen.

The rituals of the borderlands often blend traditions from different cultures, reflecting the diverse histories of those who pass through. In one instance, a curandera from Chiapas offered a limpia to a Honduran family, using plants native to southern Mexico but singing a hymn she learned from a Salvadoran refugee. This blending of traditions creates a shared spiritual language, turning the borderlands into a place of cultural convergence and mutual healing.

A BORDERLAND HEALING: TESTIMONIO OF DOÑA CARMEN

The boy clung to his mother's skirt as they stood in the dim light of the shelter. His eyes were red from crying, his small body trembling with fever. The mother's face was a mask of exhaustion, her voice breaking as she explained their journey: three weeks of walking, nights spent under makeshift tents, days with little food or water.

Doña Carmen, the curandera, knelt before the boy and placed her hands gently on his forehead. "You have carried much, pequeño," she murmured. From her woven basket, she took out a handful of ruda and crushed the leaves in her palm. The sharp scent filled the air as she rubbed the crushed herbs onto the boy's chest, her voice low with prayer. As the mother held her son close, doña Carmen glanced at the flickering candlelight. Her hands, callused from years of harvesting ruda and grinding corn, trembled with the weight of each prayer she had offered that week. "We are all crossing," she murmured to herself, "whether land, water, or the thresholds of the spirit."

"Madre Tierra, take his burden," she whispered. "Let the roots draw out his fear; let the wind carry away his pain." As the ritual unfolded, the boy's mother watched with a mixture of hope and trepidation. Doña Carmen's hands, weathered by decades of tending the land and healing the sick, moved with quiet confidence. To the mother, this moment was more than a prayer for her child—it was a lifeline, a reminder that even amid the uncertainty of migration, the sacred remained within reach. When the boy's breathing steadied, her tears fell not just from relief but because of the rediscovery of faith in something greater.

Doña Carmen took an egg and moved it in slow circles over the boy's body, absorbing the negative energy she could feel lingering in his small frame. As the ritual ended, the boy's breathing steadied and his eyes began to close. The mother wept, holding him close as doña Carmen placed a talisman in her hands—a small bundle of herbs wrapped in cloth. "This will protect him," she said. "And you too."

That night, as the boy slept, the mother lit a candle at the shelter's altar. Its flickering light illuminated offerings left by others: a handful of corn kernels, a string of rosary beads, a photo of a smiling child. In this shared space, surrounded by strangers, she found a fragile but unyielding hope.

THE BORDER'S BREATH

En las fronteras, el viento lleva historias,
de los que cruzaron, de los que quedaron.
In the borderlands, the wind carries stories,
of those who crossed, of those who stayed.

El polvo guarda huellas,
pisadas de esperanza y miedo,
de madres que susurran oraciones a la luna,
de niños que sueñan con cielos sin barreras.
The dust holds footprints,
steps of hope and fear,
of mothers whispering prayers to the moon,
of children dreaming of skies without barriers.

Pero las fronteras no son sólo líneas.
Son cicatrices, pero también son puentes.
They are scars, but they are also bridges.
Son los lugares donde el cielo se encuentra con la tierra,
donde las raíces se abrazan a pesar de las grietas.
They are places where the sky meets the earth,
where roots cling together despite the cracks.

Somos semillas que flotan en el viento,
llevadas por tormentas pero sembradas por esperanza.
We are seeds carried by storms but planted by hope.

Cada lágrima que cae riega la tierra,
cada oración que se eleva fortalece el espíritu.
Every tear that falls waters the earth,
every prayer that rises strengthens the spirit.

Las fronteras respiran, y en su aliento hay vida.
The borders breathe, and in their breath there is life.
Hay canciones que cruzan montañas,
hay fuegos que arden en la noche.
There are songs that cross mountains,
there are fires that burn in the night.

Madre Tierra, tus hijos no te han olvidado.
Earth Mother, your children have not forgotten you.
Caminamos con tus estrellas como guía,
con tus ríos como consuelo,
con tus montañas como fuerza.
We walk with your stars as our guide,
with your rivers as our comfort,
with your mountains as our strength.

Donde otros ven división, vemos unión.
Where others see division, we see unity.
Donde otros ven límites, vemos posibilidades.
Where others see boundaries, we see possibilities.

Nuestras almas no conocen fronteras,
nuestro amor no reconoce límites.
Our souls know no borders,
our love recognizes no limits.

Somos los que cruzan,
los que construyen,
los que recuerdan.
We are the ones who cross,
the ones who build,
the ones who remember.

Las mariposas cruzan sin mapas,
guiadas por memorias de viento y sol.
Butterflies cross without maps,
guided by memories of wind and sun.
Las dunas cambian, pero nunca desaparecen,
como nuestros espíritus que resisten el tiempo.
The dunes shift, but they never vanish,
like our spirits that resist the tides of time.

En las fronteras, el polvo y el viento se encuentran,
y en ese encuentro, encontramos sanación.
In the borderlands, dust and wind meet,
and in that meeting, we find healing.

• • •

The curandera's work in the borderlands is a testament to the enduring power of connection. Her rituals, prayers, and remedies remind us that borders, though imposed, cannot contain the sacred. Through her hands, the fractured land becomes whole, the displaced find roots, and the spirit reclaims its home. The borderlands are not merely lines drawn by history's conquerors; they are spaces where the sacred endures, where the resilience of those who cross weaves a tapestry of survival and connection. The curandera's voice rises above the noise of division, reminding us that the land remembers and heals. In the spaces where dust meets wind and fear meets hope, she works tirelessly to reclaim borderlands not as scars of separation but as sites of sacred renewal. Her prayers are whispers carried by the breath of the border, calling us to remember that healing is not just survival—it is revolution.

As curanderas navigate the spiritual and emotional wounds of displacement, their healing work often includes rituals of cleansing and renewal. These practices, such as limpias, connect the individual to the sacred and provide restoration amid turmoil. Chapter 4 delves into these spiritual rituals, exploring how curanderas use prayer, altars, and sacred tools to purify and heal the spirit.

CHAPTER 4

LIMPIANDO THE SPIRIT

OPENING INVOCATION

Te llamo desde las sombras del alma,
desde los lugares donde el dolor se esconde.
I call to you from the shadows of the soul,
from the places where pain hides.

Donde los caminos se cruzan entre lo visto y lo invisible,
allí está el poder de la curandera.
Where paths cross between the seen and the unseen,
there lies the power of the curandera.

Somos las que limpian con hierbas y fuego,
las que borran el miedo con rezos y esperanza.
We are the ones who cleanse with herbs and fire,
who erase fear with prayers and hope.

Con nuestras manos, tocamos las heridas invisibles,
las marcas de la historia y los ecos de la conquista.
With our hands, we touch invisible wounds,
the scars of history and the echoes of conquest.

Caminamos con el espíritu de nuestras abuelas,
con las estrellas guiando nuestras noches,
con las cenizas de lo perdido fertilizando lo que florece.
We walk with the spirit of our grandmothers,
with the stars guiding our nights,
with the ashes of what is lost fertilizing what blooms.

El espíritu no se pierde; sólo espera ser recordado.
The spirit is never lost; it only waits to be remembered.

Te llamo, porque el espíritu necesita sanar.
Te invito, porque juntos somos más fuertes.
I call to you, because the spirit needs healing.
I invite you, because together we are stronger.

RITUALS OF CLEANSING

The limpia ritual, at its core, is an ancient practice of renewal. The limpia is not simply a ritual for the individual—it is a communal and ancestral act. Oral histories from the Sierra Madre region of Mexico describe how entire families would undergo limpias before major life events, such as planting seasons or marriages, to ensure collective harmony. For these communities, cleansing the spirit was inseparable from maintaining the health of the land and relationships. By addressing the unseen forces believed to cause imbalance, curanderas reinforced the interconnectedness of all aspects of life, teaching that spiritual well-being was both a personal and a communal responsibility. The limpia bridges the physical, emotional, and spiritual worlds, uniting them in a sacred act of purification. For centuries, curanderas have used limpias to address illnesses that cannot be seen, wounds carried in the heart, and burdens that linger in the soul.

Limpias are more than spiritual acts; they are responses to historical and cultural disruptions. During the colonial era, when Indigenous rituals were banned under penalty of death, limpias became acts of quiet defiance. Across Mesoamerica, including regions such as Oaxaca and Chiapas, curanderas wove Catholic imagery into their rituals, hiding the essence of precolonial practices beneath layers of rosaries and prayers to saints. This blending of traditions allowed them to preserve ancestral knowledge while navigating the oppressive constraints of colonial rule.

In the Americas, enslaved African communities brought their own cleansing rituals, often blending them with Indigenous traditions. For example, the use of herbal baths in Afro-Caribbean spirituality combined with the Maya limpia to create new, hybrid practices that persist today in regions like Veracruz.

In precolonial Mesoamerica, limpias were central to maintaining harmony. The Nahua ticitl—the healers—conducted them at communal gatherings, using obsidian blades to symbolically cut out negative energy or obsidian mirrors to reflect harmful spirits back to their origins. The Codex Mendoza, an early colonial text, mentions Indigenous purification rituals that included the use of water, copal, and herbs, reflecting practices that date back millennia.

The tools of a limpia are never chosen at random. Each item carries its own spiritual essence.

The egg limpia, in which the egg is used as a tool for spiritual absorption, is used in varying forms across Latin America. In the Peruvian highlands, the egg is buried in earth mixed with coca leaves, symbolizing a return of negative energy to Pachamama. In Mexico, it is cracked into water, where its patterns are read like an oracle, revealing the seeker's burdens.

The herbal limpia varies widely depending on geography. In desert borderlands, sage and ocotillo are commonly used. In humid, tropical regions, curanderas may employ plants like guayusa or yerba buena. These adaptations speak to the deep relationship between curanderas and their environment—a dynamic dialogue between healer and land.

Copal smoke is a gift to the heavens that purifies the air and lifts prayers to the divine.

Among the Maya, curanderas blend the items used in the limpia with rituals tied to the sacred Tzolk'in calendar. Certain days are believed to be especially potent for releasing heavy energy, aligning the limpia with cosmic rhythms. For curanderas in contemporary urban areas, the practice often incorporates modern tools like agua florida while maintaining its ancient roots. A limpia is both deeply personal and profoundly communal. It honors the unseen struggles of an individual while connecting them to the collective strength of their ancestors and the earth itself.

THE SYMBOLISM OF THE ALTAR

At the heart of every limpia is the altar, a sacred space where the spiritual and physical converge. It is more than a physical structure—it is a map of the cosmos, a mirror of the seeker's soul, and a sanctuary for the curandera's work.

Altars are deeply personal yet share universal elements:

Water: Representing clarity and emotion, often in a small clay bowl.
Fire: A candle burning steadily, its flame a guide between worlds.
Earth: Herbs, stones, or soil, symbolizing stability and grounding.
Air: Incense or copal smoke, rising to carry prayers.

Altars serve as more than physical spaces; they are repositories of memory. Altars also reflect the curandera's adaptability in the face of change. In times of upheaval and displacement—such as the forced relocations of Indigenous peoples, or during the Mexican Revolution, when families were forced to abandon their homes—curanderas created portable altars from everyday objects: a small vial of river water, a single corn husk, a piece of flint stone, or a small bundle of herbs tied in cloth. These altars carried the essence of the sacred into unfamiliar lands, reminding families that spiritual strength was not confined to a physical place. Such practices ensured that even in times of upheaval, the connection to ancestors and the divine remained unbroken.

In contemporary urban settings, the altar's form shifts but its purpose remains unchanged. A city curandera might place subway tickets alongside sacred herbs, acknowledging the rhythms of modern life while connecting them to ancestral traditions.

The altar is not static. Each object is imbued with intention. A candle might represent clarity during confusion, but when placed beside a river stone, it symbolizes the seeker's desire for emotional grounding. The altar's meaning evolves with the needs of those it serves, reflecting the curandera's deep empathy and adaptability.

In the Mixtec highlands, curanderas build altars with regional materials like cempasúchil petals and woven palm crosses. Along the Andes, coca leaves are offered in threes, representing the sacred trilogy of past, present, and future.

The altar is also a place of storytelling. Each object holds a story: the feather placed to honor a bird's sacrifice, the stone carried from a sacred river, the candle lit with a whispered intention. These stories become part of the seeker's healing, reminding them that they are part of a larger, ongoing narrative.

HEALING THE SPIRIT, HEALING THE LAND

For the curandera, the health of the spirit is inextricably tied to the health of the land. Tonantzin, the earth mother, is not just a giver of life but a carrier of wounds. Just as the body carries the memory of pain, so too does the land carry the weight of colonization, deforestation, and disconnection.

Rituals of healing often extend beyond the individual to the earth itself. In the Cañada de los Once Pueblos in Michoacán, curanderas perform ceremonies to heal damaged rivers. They pour agua florida and scatter flower petals, chanting prayers to ask the spirits of the water for forgiveness and renewal. In the Andes, ceremonies dedicated to Pachamama involve burying offerings of food and drink, an act of reciprocity for the earth's nourishment.

The limpia, in this context, becomes an act of resistance. It defies the commodification of both land and spirit by reaffirming their sacredness. Every herb gathered, every prayer spoken, is a reminder that healing is not just survival—it is reclamation. Environmental healing rituals often echo ancient Indigenous practices rooted in reciprocity. In Chiapas, for example, curanderas perform ceremonies to cleanse polluted rivers, using wildflowers and tobacco leaves as offerings to the water spirits. Archival records from the National Museum of Anthropology in Mexico City describe similar ceremonies in which curanderas invoked Tlaloc, the rain god, to heal drought-stricken fields. These acts, steeped in reverence, remind communities that healing the land is both a spiritual obligation and a means of restoring balance to human lives. By mending the wounds of the earth, curanderas reaffirm humanity's sacred relationship with nature.

A DAY IN THE LIFE OF A CURANDERA PERFORMING A LIMPIA: TESTIMONIO OF BERNA

The sun rose quietly over the outskirts of Mexicali, casting a soft golden light over the dry earth and low hills. The air carried the faint scent of sagebrush and the lingering freshness of an early rain. Berna, a revered curandera, began her day as she always did—with a small offering at her altar. At the center of the altar stood a statue of the Santo Niño de Atocha, dressed in his iconic pilgrim attire, a symbol of protection and guidance. Surrounding him were candles, a handful of maize, and a small bowl of fresh water. "Gracias, Santo Niño," she whispered, her voice steady. "Guíanos en este día."

At mid-morning, a man arrived at her door, his shoulders slumped under the weight of invisible burdens. He had been unemployed for months and felt a suffocating sense of despair that he could not shake. Berna greeted him with a calm nod and motioned for him to sit. She listened without interruption as he spoke, her hands moving with practiced care to prepare the tools of the limpia: a fresh egg, a bundle of ruda, and a small bottle of agua de rosas she had prepared the night before.

"Stand here," she said, gesturing to a woven mat laid before her altar. The man rose slowly, his exhaustion evident in his sluggish movements.

Berna began by lighting copal in a small clay censer, the fragrant smoke curling upward like a protective shield. Holding the egg in one hand, she swept it over the man's body, moving in deliberate, circular motions. Her voice rose and fell in rhythmic chants: "Santo Niño de Atocha, intercede por este hijo tuyo. Madre Tonantzin, limpia su camino, fortalece su espíritu." The egg, cool and smooth in her hand, grew heavier with each pass, as though absorbing the sorrow and fear that clung to him.

When the ritual was complete, Berna carefully cracked the egg into a shallow bowl of water. The yolk swirled into intricate patterns, its shapes telling a deeper story. "This is not just your burden," she said, her voice soft but firm. "It is the weight of your father's struggles and his father's before him. Pain carried through generations." She took the bowl outside to the patch of desert sage growing near her home. Kneeling, she poured its contents into the soil, whispering a prayer to release the burdens into the earth, where they could be transformed.

Returning to the man, Berna reached into a small basket by her altar and pulled out a bundle of ruda and rosemary, tied with a strand of red thread. "Burn the ruda in your home to cleanse the air," she said. "Steep the rosemary in water and bathe with it to keep your spirit light. And pray to the Santo Niño. Ask him to guide you on your path and give you strength."

As the man left, his steps lighter and his shoulders less burdened, Berna lingered by her altar. She placed a small offering of bread and water before the Santo Niño de Atocha, bowing her head in gratitude. Outside, the sun climbed higher, warming the earth as the winds carried her whispered prayers far beyond the horizon.

THE SPIRIT REMEMBERS

El espíritu recuerda, aunque tú olvides,
los cantos de la tierra, los susurros del viento.
The spirit remembers, even if you forget,
the songs of the earth, the whispers of the wind.

En cada hoja de ruda, en cada grano de maíz,
vive la memoria de quienes vinieron antes.
In every leaf of rue, in every kernel of maize,
lives the memory of those who came before.

No olvides el poder de tus manos,
capaces de sanar lo que parecía perdido.
Do not forget the power of your hands,
capable of healing what once seemed lost.

Cuando el mundo te pese,
recuerda que el fuego de tus ancestros aún arde.
When the world weighs on you,
remember that your ancestors' fire still burns.

Con cada rezo, reconstruimos lo que fue quebrado.
Con cada limpia, sembramos un futuro más fuerte.

With every prayer, we rebuild what was broken.
With every cleansing, we plant a stronger future.

El espíritu nunca se pierde;
siempre encuentra el camino de regreso.
The spirit is never lost;
it always finds its way back.

Y en ese regreso, encontramos nuestra fuerza.
And in that return, we find our strength.

• • •

The limpia is more than a ritual; it is an invitation to remember. It calls us to reconnect with the sacred, to honor the land that sustains us, and to trust in the resilience of the human spirit. In the hands of the curandera, healing becomes a quiet revolution, a reclamation of what colonization sought to erase. Through her work, the spirit is not just cleansed but awakened, ready to walk once more in harmony with the earth and the ancestors who guide it. Healing is not just an act—it is a legacy. The spirit's memory is not bound by time or place. It carries the echoes of prayers whispered in forgotten languages and the wisdom of rituals performed beneath ancient skies. As curanderas awaken this memory through their work, they remind us that healing is a return to wholeness—not just for the individual but for the generations before and after. Each limpia, each prayer, becomes a thread in the tapestry of collective resilience, ensuring that the knowledge of the past continues to guide the path forward.

Chapter 5 turns toward the land as a central site of curanderismo practice and knowledge production. Rather than treating healing as an abstract or purely interpersonal process, this chapter situates curanderismo within sustained relationships to place, territory, and the natural elements.

CHAPTER 5

FROM MADRE TIERRA WE RISE

OPENING INVOCATION

Te llamo desde las entrañas de la montaña,
desde los vientos que arrastran semillas de esperanza.
I call to you from the depths of the mountain,
from the winds that carry seeds of hope.

Donde el fuego se encuentra con el agua,
y las raíces abrazan las estrellas,
nacemos de nuevo.
Where fire meets water,
and roots embrace the stars,
we are born anew.

Somos los hijos de la tierra,
los que escuchan el murmullo de los volcanes,
los que bailan con la lluvia y cantan con el río.
We are the children of the earth,
those who listen to the murmurs of volcanoes,
those who dance with the rain and sing with the river.

En el barro está nuestra memoria,
y en las cenizas está nuestra fuerza.
In the clay lies our memory,
and in the ashes lies our strength.

Madre Tierra, somos tus manos que plantan,
tus pies que cruzan caminos,
tu aliento que da vida a los sueños.
Mother Earth, we are your planting hands,
your feet that cross paths,
your breath that gives life to dreams.

Te llamo, porque juntos
podemos renacer en armonía contigo.
I call to you, because together
we can be reborn in harmony with you.

• • •

This invocation reminds us that the earth's wisdom flows through us, shaping our healing practices and anchoring us in its infinite cycles. It is both a call to Madre Tierra and a reminder of the sacred relationship we are called to nurture. Listening is not a passive act—it requires courage and humility. A curandera kneels before the earth, pressing her palms into the soil as though seeking its heartbeat. "What do you need?" she asks, her voice barely above a whisper. In her silence, she hears the answer: the land needs care, just as she needs its guidance. This reciprocal relationship becomes a sacred dialogue, where every offering—whether a prayer, a seed, or a handful of water—is both a gift and a promise to protect the bond between humanity and the earth.

THE EARTH AS OUR TEACHER

The earth is more than a provider of life; it is the keeper of ancient lessons. For centuries, curanderas have drawn their strength and wisdom from observing the land's cycles—its resilience after storms, its patience in waiting for spring, its ability to heal after fire. These lessons remind us that healing is not instantaneous but a journey, one deeply rooted in reciprocity and respect.

In precolonial times, the Nahua people referred to the earth as Tlalli Tonantzin—Mother Earth. Rituals dedicated to her honored the interconnectedness of life. Farmers would leave offerings at planting season, knowing that their crops relied on her nourishment. Midwives invoked her strength during childbirth, comparing a mother's labor to the earth's labor in bringing forth life.

During the spring planting season, Nahua farmers held festivals honoring Tlalli Tonantzin, offering tamales and pulque (a traditional and ritual drink made from fermented agave syrup) at the base of sacred mountains. These rituals emphasized the earth's dual role as mother and provider, drawing parallels between the cycles of agriculture and human life. For the Mayas in the Yucatán, cenotes were not just sources of water but portals to the underworld, where offerings of jade and maize were placed to ensure balance between the human and divine realms.

While the rituals of the Nahua and Maya communities illustrate a historical reverence for Madre Tierra, this relationship remains alive today, adapting to the challenges of modern life. Across regions, curanderas continue to embody the lessons of the earth, weaving ancient wisdom into contemporary practices.

These traditions continue. Along the Andes, ceremonies dedicated to Pachamama involve the burying of coca leaves and maize, symbolizing gratitude and balance. In the deserts of the Sonoran borderlands, Indigenous communities weave prayers into the wind, trusting the earth to carry their words. In the Caribbean, curanderas known as yerberas incorporate ocean water and tropical plants like guanábana leaves into their healing rituals. In urban settings, curanderas adapt their practices to the limited access to natural materials. Rooftop gardens, repurposed household items, and digital sharing of rituals through social media are becoming common ways to keep these traditions alive. This innovation reflects the enduring resilience of curanderismo, bridging ancient wisdom with modern life.

In the Andean highlands, yatiris, Aymara healers, honor the spirit of the condor, whose flight represents freedom and vision, by using feathers in ceremonial cleansings. These regional practices, while distinct, share a common reverence for the elements and a belief that healing is a reciprocal exchange between humans and the natural world.

For the curandera, the earth's resilience becomes her own. Berna, the curandera in Mexicali described in the previous chapter, often said, "The earth gives us what we need, but it asks for care in return." This wisdom guided her practice, whether she was tending to her small garden of sage and ruda or leading a planting ceremony in the fields outside Mexicali. Her rituals were simple yet profound: a handful of maize kernels buried in the soil with whispered prayers, a small bowl of water poured at the base of plants during droughts. For her, these acts of reciprocity were essential to maintaining the balance between humans and the land, a lesson she insisted could not be forgotten. Each herb she gathers, each stone she blesses, reminds her that healing begins by listening—to the land, to the self, and to the spirits that guide us. Just as roots anchor a tree to the earth while reaching unseen depths, the lessons of Madre Tierra ground us while connecting us to the ancestors and spirits who guide our healing. The curandera reminds us that in nurturing these roots, we find the strength to weather any storm and the wisdom to grow anew. This reciprocity extends beyond the individual to the collective. Just as the earth gives unconditionally, we are called to care for it in return. Communities practicing curanderismo often organize collective clean-ups of rivers or replant native species, reinforcing the idea that healing the land heals us all.

HEALING THROUGH THE FOUR ELEMENTS

Curanderas often work with the elements—earth, water, fire, and air—not only as metaphors but as active participants in the healing process. Each element carries its own energy and message, serving as a bridge between the physical and spiritual realms.

Earth: Grounding and Stability

The earth grounds us when the world feels unstable. In rituals, curanderas may use clay masks or mud baths to draw toxins from the body, exhibiting the earth's ability to absorb and transform. Stones from sacred rivers are placed on altars, anchoring the seeker to their lineage and reminding them of the unbroken connection between past and present.

Water: Cleansing and Renewal

Water flows through every limpia, whether sprinkled from a palm leaf or poured into the soil as an offering. In Mayan ceremonies, sacred cenotes are used for spiritual baptisms; seekers are immersed in waters believed to connect directly to the underworld and the divine. Curanderas blend water with herbs like lavender and basil, creating infusions that soothe the spirit and cleanse the body.

Fire: Transformation and Strength

Fire, like the curandera, is a force of duality—capable of destruction yet essential for renewal. The burning of copal during rituals represents both cleansing and communication with the divine. In the Mixtec tradition, fire is seen as a sacred intermediary, carrying prayers to the heavens and illuminating the seeker's path.

Air: Movement and Freedom

Air reminds us to let go. The blowing of smoke over a seeker during a limpia represents the release of stagnant energy. Feathers, often used in ceremonies, guide the movement of this energy, symbolizing lightness and the ability to rise above challenges.

• • •

Through the elements, the curandera weaves a holistic healing process, addressing not only the physical body but the emotional and spiritual landscapes as well. Yet the elements themselves are not isolated forces—they exist in harmony, reflecting the interconnectedness of life. A cleansing with water often begins by grounding the seeker with earth, while fire and air carry away what no longer serves them. Abuela Berna's rituals often wove all four elements into a single act of healing. During a limpia for a young mother struggling with grief, she began by sprinkling water infused with rosemary and ruda over the woman's hands and feet, asking the earth to ground her. Next, she lit a small bundle of sage, fanning the smoke with a bird feather to symbolize air's ability to carry away sorrow. Finally, she placed a burning candle at the altar, the flame representing the transformation of pain into strength. "The elements work together as we do," she explained, "each supporting the other to bring balance."

In one ritual, a curandera from Oaxaca combined all four elements: she buried herbs in the earth to anchor the seeker's intentions, sprinkled water infused with basil over their hands, lit a candle to burn away fear, and used a feather to fan the smoke upward, releasing it into the air. "The elements work together," she explained. "You cannot separate them, just as you cannot separate the body, mind, and spirit."

A STORY OF RESILIENCE: TESTIMONIO OF DOÑA ESPERANZA

It was midday when doña Esperanza began her ritual on the shores of Lake Atitlán in Guatemala. A family had arrived, seeking her guidance after a year of drought had ravaged their crops. The parents carried their worry like stones on their shoulders, and their youngest child clung to their legs, her eyes wide with unspoken fears.

Doña Esperanza started by gathering lake water in a clay bowl, adding petals of marigold and a pinch of salt. She dipped a bundle of sage into the water, whispering prayers to the spirit of the lake. "Madre Tierra, escucha nuestras súplicas," she murmured. "Mother Earth, hear our pleas."

The family watched as she sprinkled the water over their hands, their foreheads, and finally the soil they had brought with them—a handful of earth from their parched fields. "This drought is a test," she said softly, "but the earth always remembers how to heal. And so do we."

As the family listened, the father's shoulders began to relax, the weight of worry visibly softening. Doña Esperanza turned to the youngest child, her voice gentle but firm. "Your hands carry the strength of your ancestors," she said, placing the child's small palms on the clay bowl filled with marigold petals. "Remember, little one, the earth is always with you, no matter where you are." For a moment, the family stood in silence, the child's fingers tracing the petals as though seeking a promise from the lake itself. Doña Esperanza smiled, knowing that hope, once planted, would grow even in the driest soil.

She handed the family a small bundle wrapped in cloth—seeds blessed with prayers for renewal. "Plant these," she said, "and tend to them as you would tend to your hope." As Doña Esperanza handed the small bundle of seeds to the family, their eyes glistened with a mixture of gratitude and hope. The father held the cloth-wrapped seeds tightly, as though they were a lifeline, while the child reached out to touch them with quiet reverence. In that moment, the seeds became more than a promise—they became a reminder that even in the harshest drought, life could begin anew. "Plant these with care," she said, her voice steady. "They hold not only the prayers of this moment but the strength of those who walked before you."

RECLAIMING THE SACRED

In a world that often views the earth as a resource to exploit, the curandera reclaims its sacredness. Each ritual becomes an act of resistance, a declaration that the land is not a commodity but a partner.

In northern Peru, a curandero named Florencio uses feathers from local hawks during limpias to guide smoke in deliberate patterns, channeling energy toward healing the heart. Similarly, in Veracruz, curanderas blend clay from sacred rivers with medicinal herbs to create poultices that symbolize the grounding strength of the earth, applied during rituals for those feeling unmoored by loss.

In regions impacted by deforestation and mining, curanderas perform ceremonies to heal the land. One such story comes from the Amazon, where a group of Indigenous women, led by a revered curandera named Ana Lluvia, stood against the encroachment of mining companies. They gathered under the shade of ancient ceiba trees, pouring sacred waters onto the roots while singing prayers for protection. The ceremony drew international attention, inspiring allies to join their fight and forcing the government to halt mining operations in the region. This act of spiritual resistance, combined with organized activism, underscored the power of curanderismo as both a ritual and a call to action. These efforts echo larger global movements like ecofeminism, which highlights the intersection of environmental sustainability and women's rights.

Curanderas like Ana Lluvia remind us that protecting the earth is inherently tied to preserving cultural identity, making their rituals both local and universal acts of justice. Ecofeminism frames this work as a response to the dual exploitation of women and the earth under colonial and capitalist systems. Curanderas reclaim the sacred by honoring both their roles as caregivers and the land's inherent value. This duality positions curanderismo as a bridge between environmental movements and social justice, a testament to the interconnectedness of all forms of life.

The curandera's rituals remind us that healing is inherently communal, connecting the individual to their environment and their community. Along the Amazon River, Indigenous women lead rituals blending curanderismo with activism, calling upon spirits to protect their waters. In Mexico, prayers to Tonantzin are offered at the base of mountains threatened by development, weaving modern struggles into ancient traditions. These acts remind us that healing is not just about the self—it is about restoring balance to the world around us. Acts of spiritual resistance, like Ana Lluvia's ceremony under the ceiba trees, transcend local struggles, weaving ancient traditions into global movements for justice. By protecting the land, curanderas protect the cultures and identities that are inseparable from it, offering a powerful testament to the resilience of both the earth and its people.

RAÍCES DE LA MEMORIA

Somos los hijos de la tierra,
los que escuchan su latido incluso en el ruido del mundo.
We are the children of the earth,
those who hear its heartbeat even in the noise of the world.

En cada semilla, hay una promesa.
En cada río, hay una canción.
In every seed, there is a promise.
In every river, there is a song.

Madre Tierra, caminamos contigo,
aunque el camino sea difícil, aunque el tiempo sea largo.
Mother Earth, we walk with you,
though the road is hard, though the journey is long.

Tú nos das raíces cuando el viento nos arranca,
tú nos das fuerza cuando el mundo nos debilita.
You give us roots when the wind pulls us away,
you give us strength when the world makes us weak.

En tu barro, reconstruimos nuestras almas.
En tu fuego, encontramos nuestra voz.
In your clay, we rebuild our souls.
In your fire, we find our voice.

Nunca olvidaremos quiénes somos,
porque en tus cenizas está nuestra memoria.
We will never forget who we are,
because in your ashes lies our memory.

• • •

This closing poem reminds us that the earth is not just a witness to our stories but an active participant in them. In the hands of the curandera, Madre Tierra's gifts—her clay, her waters, her winds—become tools for healing and remembering. As we honor the earth, we also honor ourselves, reclaiming the strength and resilience that lie buried in her roots and in our own. In this harmony, the curandera teaches us that healing is not only possible but inevitable, as long as we walk with the earth by our side. The poem's imagery roots us in the intimate relationship between humanity and the earth, calling forth a shared strength and resilience that transcends borders, wounds, and time. It reminds us that even in moments of displacement or destruction, the earth holds our stories, offering its elements as tools for healing and growth. The declaration that we are infinite is both an affirmation of collective power and a promise to carry forward the lessons of the land. In this way, the curandera's work becomes not just a practice of restoration but a legacy of remembering, inviting all of us to find our own harmony with Madre Tierra.

As curanderismo evolves, it also continues to thrive across diasporic communities. These practices transcend geographic boundaries, blending with local traditions while maintaining cultural roots. Chapter 6 examines how curanderismo flourishes in diasporas, offering a bridge between heritage and adaptation.

CHAPTER 6

CURANDERISMO ACROSS DIASPORAS

OPENING INVOCATION

Te llamo desde la tierra de la diáspora,
desde los lugares donde nuestras raíces han sido arrancadas
pero seguimos floreciendo.
I call to you from the land of the diaspora,
from the places where our roots have been uprooted
but we continue to bloom.

Somos los hijos de la migración,
los que cruzamos fronteras
pero nunca olvidamos nuestra tierra madre.
We are the children of migration,
the ones who cross borders
but never forget our motherland.

Cargamos en nuestras manos las semillas de la esperanza,
y en nuestro pecho, la memoria de nuestras abuelas.
We carry in our hands the seeds of hope,
and in our chest, the memory of our grandmothers.

Donde el sol brilla distinto
y las montañas se ven a lo lejos,
nos encontramos, siempre buscando regresar a casa.
Where the sun shines differently
and the mountains are seen from afar,
we find ourselves, always seeking to return home.

Te llamo, porque aunque nos hayan dispersado,
somos uno, en espíritu y en tierra.
I call to you, because though we have been scattered,
we are one, in spirit and in earth.

• • •

This invocation calls to the heart of the diaspora, where the practice of curanderismo becomes both a lifeline and a bridge. It reminds us that while migration may scatter us, it cannot sever the sacred bond between healer, land, and spirit.

CURANDERISMO ACROSS BORDERS

Curanderismo, with its deeply rooted ties to Indigenous practices and spiritual healing, has crossed borders in the diaspora. The migration of curanderismo is intricately tied to the historical movements of Latinx communities across borders. During the Mexican Revolution, families fleeing violence carried their healing traditions with them into the U.S. Southwest, where curanderas adapted their practices to desert landscapes and border towns. Each migration carried not only the physical tools of curanderismo—herbs, candles, and sacred objects—but also the spirit of survival and adaptation. Curanderas like María Luisa, who crossed the border during the Mexican Revolution, found new ways to create healing spaces in unfamiliar landscapes. In the desert towns of Arizona, they transformed their surroundings into sanctuaries, using the resilience of the land to mirror the resilience of their people.

Later, during the Bracero Program of the mid-twentieth century, migrant workers brought remedies and rituals to California's agricultural valleys, establishing networks of healing within labor camps. These migrations did not dilute curanderismo; rather, they strengthened its role as a source of resilience and cultural preservation in the face of displacement. For generations, curanderas have carried with them their knowledge of plants, rituals, and sacred traditions as they migrated, whether across the Americas or beyond, bringing their healing arts to new places. But this migration, both physical and cultural, has not been without challenges. In unfamiliar lands, curanderas have had to adapt while holding tight to their ancestral wisdom.

In cities like Los Angeles, New York, and Miami, curanderas continue to practice their craft, often working in communities of Latinx and Indigenous migrants. These urban landscapes become home to sacred rituals and healing spaces that serve as a refuge for the displaced. Just as they have done for centuries, curanderas bring plants like ruda, epazote, and yerba santa from their homelands to create altars and perform limpias, but they also begin to blend their knowledge with new traditions.

In the midst of the diaspora, curanderas may now use modern-day tools such as essential oils or urban herbs alongside the traditional herbs of their homelands. But whether in the mountains of Guatemala or the streets of Los Angeles, their spiritual work remains the same: the healing of individuals, families, and communities.

Curanderismo offers a framework for addressing modern ecological crises. The practice of gathering herbs with ritualized respect is a powerful counternarrative to exploitative agricultural practices. In Oaxaca, communities advocate for sustainable harvesting of sage and copal, ensuring these sacred plants remain abundant for future generations. Additionally, curanderismo highlights the importance of ecological reciprocity. Ceremonies to honor rain spirits, such as those performed by Maya daykeepers, teach reverence for natural cycles. These practices serve as a blueprint for modern movements seeking to reconnect humanity with the earth.

ADAPTING HEALING PRACTICES

Healing practices must evolve when curanderas move to new environments, but adaptation does not mean abandoning their roots. In urban environments, curanderas find sacredness in unexpected places. Community gardens become sites of ritual, where plants like sage and lavender are cultivated alongside vegetables, providing both physical and spiritual nourishment. Public parks offer spaces for limpias, where the rustling of leaves replaces the winds of the open fields back home. In immigrant neighborhoods, curanderas bless thresholds with copal smoke, transforming apartments into sanctuaries. These practices remind the displaced that sacredness is not bound to geography but lives in the relationships we build with the land, no matter where we are. It means finding new ways to integrate the land and spirit of their new home while keeping the practices that connect them to the earth and their ancestors alive.

Curanderas in urban areas have learned to transform their surroundings and to use what is available to them: the plants that grow in their gardens, the stones that line the sidewalks, and the water that flows through urban canals. These new environments become sacred spaces, holding their own power and spirit, ready to be tapped for healing. In Toronto, for instance, curanderas have taken the practice of creating protective bundles for their families—common in rural areas in Mexico—and adapted it to the urban environment. They use city herbs, like lavender and mint, and pair them with symbols from both their Indigenous traditions and Catholic iconography. Curanderas who have migrated to Spain lead healing circles that incorporate Mediterranean plants. This blending of old and new creates healing rituals that honor the land, wherever it may be, and the community that inhabits it.

In Canada, curanderas collaborate with First Nations communities, exchanging knowledge about plant medicines and rituals tied to land stewardship. In London, Latinx healers have organized wellness circles that blend curanderismo with global traditions, incorporating Ayurvedic practices and African diasporic spirituality. These cross-cultural exchanges do not dilute curanderismo but expand its reach, creating new pathways for healing while honoring its ancestral roots.

In the digital age, curanderas are finding new ways to connect with diasporic communities. Social media platforms serve as virtual altars where healers share herbal recipes, prayers, and rituals with followers across continents. Online workshops and healing circles bring together participants from distant lands, creating a shared sacred space despite physical separation. This digital dissemination ensures that curanderismo remains accessible, adapting to modern realities while staying deeply rooted in tradition.

By bridging traditions across continents, curanderas demonstrate that their work transcends borders, uniting communities through shared reverence for the sacred. The land that once felt foreign to them becomes a sacred space in which to heal, to create altars, and to offer spiritual protection to families who feel displaced. Just as the Mediterranean plants are used in new ways, these curanderas also adapt their rituals to the context of migration, not only using traditional knowledge but also incorporating contemporary healing practices to create safe spaces.

HEALING THE SOUL AND SPIRIT

Curanderismo across the diaspora is not just about addressing the physical ailments of migrants; it's also about the deep spiritual healing necessary when one is displaced. Whether they are separated from family, homeland, or heritage, migrants often experience what curanderas call "soul wounds." These are the emotional and spiritual scars left by the trauma of migration: the pain of leaving, the uncertainty of arrival, and the longing to return.

In Los Angeles, California, a group of curanderas organizes monthly gatherings for immigrants grieving the loss of their homeland. At a recent gathering, doña Luz led a ceremony where participants placed candles and handwritten prayers in a circle of marigolds. As the curanderas chanted, the group shared their stories, tears falling freely. "This is not just about healing one person," doña Luz explained. "It's about mending the invisible threads that connect us all." These ceremonies remind participants that their pain is seen, their ancestors are remembered, and their spirits are held in a community of care.

In places like Chile and Peru, curanderas adapt their practices by holding community gatherings in which they perform rituals for healing the soul. These gatherings are spiritual acts of resistance, turning community spaces into places of remembrance, where ancestral knowledge and healing can be shared. Curanderas invite the community to come together to help heal the wounds of migration and colonialism, using rituals of remembrance to call back the spirits of their ancestors.

In Mexico, curanderas have expanded their role as community healers to become leaders in social justice, using their knowledge of the sacred to challenge the systems that perpetuate injustice. Curanderas have become pivotal figures in grassroots movements, blending spiritual rituals with calls for justice. During immigration protests in Los Angeles, curanderas led processions, burning copal and chanting prayers for protection over demonstrators. Similarly, in Arizona, a collective of curanderas supported migrants at detention centers, offering spiritual cleansings to those recently released. These acts underscore the dual role of curanderismo as both a healing practice and a form of resistance, affirming that justice for the body and for the soul are deeply interconnected.

The influence of curanderismo has reached far beyond Latinx communities, inspiring shared resonances. Practitioners in Africa, Asia, and Europe have drawn from its emphasis on holistic wellness and connection to the earth. In Australia, Indigenous healers have engaged with curanderas to exchange knowledge about sacred plants and rituals, fostering cross-cultural dialogues that highlight shared struggles and strengths. These interactions underscore the universal power of ancestral healing, rooted in the earth and carried through generations.

The influence of curanderismo has reached far beyond Latinx communities, inspiring global healing movements. In Africa, traditional healers in Ghana have drawn parallels between curanderismo and their own herbal medicine practices, emphasizing shared values of holistic wellness and community care. During a healing exchange in Accra, a curandera shared the use of copal for spiritual cleansing while learning about the protective properties of shea butter, creating a dialogue between traditions rooted in land and ancestry.

In Asia, curanderismo has resonated with practitioners of Ayurveda in India, who recognize the commonalities between their approaches to balance and energy flow. A curandera from Peru, visiting Kerala, marveled at the similarities in the use of basil—known as tulsi in India—as a sacred herb for protection and healing. These exchanges foster mutual respect and highlight the universality of ancestral wisdom.

In Australia, Indigenous healers and curanderas have come together in ceremonies that honor the sacredness of water. During a gathering near the Murray River, an Aboriginal elder shared the tradition of "singing to the water" to heal its spirit, while a curandera performed a limpia using local eucalyptus leaves. This blending of rituals reflects a shared understanding of the earth as a living entity that holds both memory and power.

These interactions underscore the universal power of ancestral healing, rooted in the earth and carried through generations. They demonstrate that while curanderismo is deeply tied to Latinx culture, its principles resonate across continents, uniting communities through shared reverence for the sacred. Curanderas work alongside activists, using their rituals to heal the wounds of oppression and displacement that plague marginalized communities.

A STORY OF RESILIENCE: TESTIMONIO OF ROSA

Curandera Rosa, a healer from Oaxaca, arrived in the United States after a long and treacherous journey. She left behind her home and the sacred mountains she had known her whole life. In the bustling streets of Los Angeles, she began to offer her services to fellow immigrants, using her knowledge of curanderismo to help heal the wounds of migration.

One day, a mother and daughter arrived at her door. The daughter had been unable to speak since their journey began, and the mother feared her silence was a result of the trauma of crossing the border. Rosa welcomed them into her space and set up an altar with flowers, candles, and small statues of saints. She gathered the herbs she knew could heal the spirit—ruda, yerba buena, and copal—and began the limpia ritual. As the smoke swirled around them, Rosa whispered a prayer to the ancestors, asking for the courage and strength to break the silence that weighed so heavily on the young girl.

The next morning, the daughter spoke for the first time since they had crossed the border, thanking the curandera for bringing peace to her heart. "It was not the earth alone that healed me," she said. "It was the love and memory of those who came before me." After the girl spoke, Rosa reflected on the power of memory and spirit in the healing process. "We carry so much pain across these borders," she said, "but the ancestors are always with us, guiding us back to wholeness." Healing is not just about what we do—it's about what we remember.

CURANDERISMO AS A LEGACY OF RESISTANCE

For curanderas in the diaspora, healing is not only an individual practice; it is a collective act of resistance. In the face of a world that often seeks to erase their history and identity, curanderas fight to keep ancestral knowledge alive, weaving it into the very fabric of their new lives. Curanderas in the diaspora understand that survival is not enough—continuity is essential. Many have taken on the role of teachers, mentoring younger generations in the art of healing. Workshops on herbal medicine, storytelling circles, and ceremonial practices are passed down as acts of cultural preservation. These teachings are not limited to those of Latinx descent; curanderas welcome those who wish to honor the land and its sacredness, cultivating a global community of learners who carry these traditions into the future. By continuing to practice curanderismo, they honor their ancestors and keep their cultures thriving. These acts of spiritual resistance extend beyond personal healing to collective restoration.

Curanderas in urban centers become beacons of light, offering rituals, herbal remedies, and spiritual guidance to migrants who need a connection to their homeland, a bridge between the old and the new. Their work, rooted in tradition, adapts to the needs of a modern, often diasporic community, making them not only healers but keepers of memory and resistance.

The legacy of curanderismo extends beyond Latinx communities, offering a blueprint for resilience and reclamation in marginalized cultures worldwide. By blending ancestral wisdom with activism, curanderas demonstrate how healing practices can serve as tools for both individual recovery and collective empowerment. This dual role inspires other communities to reclaim their own healing traditions as acts of cultural preservation and resistance.

UNION DE RAÍCES

Y cuando el mundo nos llame pequeños,
levantaremos nuestras manos llenas de tierra y diremos:
somos infinitos.
And when the world calls us small,
we will raise our hands filled with earth and say:
we are infinite.

Las estrellas nos miran desde el principio de los tiempos,
recordándonos que somos polvo cósmico y raíz terrenal.

The stars watch us from the beginning of time,
reminding us that we are cosmic dust and earthly root.

Cuando cantamos con el río, nuestras voces se mezclan
con los ecos de los ancestros que nunca se han ido.
When we sing with the river, our voices blend
with the echoes of ancestors who have never left.

Madre Tierra, somos tus hijos y tus guerreros,
tus sembradores de esperanza en un mundo herido.
Mother Earth, we are your children and your warriors,
your sowers of hope in a wounded world.

Y en el polvo de los caminos,
donde las fronteras intentan dividirnos,
encontramos nuestra unión más profunda.
And in the dust of the roads,
where borders try to divide us,
we find our deepest union.

No somos ramas separadas,
somos un solo árbol,
creciendo hacia el cielo con raíces infinitas.
We are not separate branches,
we are one tree,
growing toward the sky with infinite roots.

• • •

This poem speaks to the heart of curanderismo in the diaspora, where roots are not lost but transformed. It reminds us that while borders may divide land, they cannot divide spirit. Through curanderismo, we reclaim our connection to the earth and to each other, affirming that even in displacement, we remain infinite—children of the earth, sowers of hope, and keepers of ancestral memory. The poem reflects the enduring power of ancestral memory and communal resilience, emphasizing the connection between identity, land, and spirit. It reminds us that curanderismo is not just a practice of healing; it is a practice of remembering—of reclaiming what migration, colonization, and separation attempt to sever. In the dust of distant roads, the waters of new lands, and the winds that carry voices across continents, we find not division but unity. This unity, born of shared roots and infinite strength, reminds us that healing is both an act of survival and a revolution of the soul.

In diasporic contexts, curanderas are not only preserving traditions but also innovating new practices that reflect diverse identities and experiences. These modern healers transform urban environments into sacred spaces, cultivating gardens and rituals that honor both tradition and change. Chapter 7 highlights the ingenuity and adaptability of this new generation of curanderas.

CHAPTER 7

NEW-GEN HEALERS

OPENING INVOCATION

Te llamo desde los tiempos modernos,
donde las llamas de las velas iluminan pantallas
y las voces de nuestros ancestros se escuchan en líneas digitales.
I call to you from modern times,
where candle flames light up screens
and the voices of our ancestors echo in digital lines.

Somos las curanderas de dos mundos,
nuestras raíces en el barro, nuestras ramas en el cielo,
sosteniendo lo eterno en un mundo que siempre cambia.
We are the curanderas of two worlds,
our roots in the clay, our branches in the sky,
holding the eternal in a world that is always changing.

Madre Tierra, aún escuchamos tu llamado,
a través del ruido de las ciudades
y los ecos digitales de nuestra voz.
Mother Earth, we still hear your call,
through the noise of cities
and the digital echoes of our voice.

En los balcones, donde crecen hierbas en macetas,
y en los tejados que se vuelven jardines sagrados,
creamos espacios para sanar, incluso entre el concreto.
On balconies where herbs grow in pots,
and rooftops that become sacred gardens,
we create spaces for healing, even among concrete.

Te llamamos con rezos en líneas de texto,
con videos que enseñan a mezclar remedios,
y con palabras que llevan raíces al futuro.
We call to you with prayers sent in text,
with videos teaching the blending of remedies,
and with words carrying roots into the future.

Somos las tejedoras de memoria,
las que iluminan el camino con copal,
y las que encuentran lo sagrado en lo cotidiano.
We are the weavers of memory,
the ones who light the way with copal,
and the ones who find the sacred in the everyday.

Porque aunque el mundo cambie
y los caminos se separen,
tu espíritu vive en nuestros corazones, eterno e indivisible.
Because even as the world changes
and paths diverge,
your spirit lives in our hearts, eternal and indivisible.

• • •

This invocation is a reminder that the essence of curanderismo is not confined to a particular time, place, or form. Whether practiced in remote villages, bustling cities, or virtual spaces, the curandera's work transcends borders and eras. It is a testament to the enduring bond between healer and earth, between ancient wisdom and modern life. As curanderas navigate the complexities of the present, they carry the echoes of their ancestors while planting seeds for future generations. This duality—rooted in tradition yet open to change—

defines the modern curandera and the sacred work she continues to offer the world.

THE EVOLUTION OF THE MODERN CURANDERA

The modern curandera walks in two worlds: the ancient and the contemporary. While her roots remain firmly grounded in ancestral knowledge, her branches stretch into the digital age and urban landscapes, and she adapts her practice to meet the needs of a rapidly changing world. She carries ruda in one hand and a smartphone in the other, bridging tradition and innovation.

Historically, curanderismo thrived in rural villages where curanderas worked closely with their natural environments. Migration changed this, as families moved to cities and other countries, taking their healing practices with them. Curanderas adapted by creating sacred spaces wherever they settled—on urban balconies, in community centers, or even within the digital realm.

Take doña Marta, who moved to Chicago from Puebla in the 1980s. Her small apartment became a gathering space for limpias and spiritual consultations. "The city doesn't have open fields," she says, "but it has people who need healing, and that's what matters." For Marta, adaptation is not a compromise—it is a continuation of curanderismo's enduring spirit.

DIGITAL HEALING: CURANDERISMO IN THE AGE OF TECHNOLOGY

Social media has become a powerful altar for the modern curandera. Platforms like Instagram, TikTok, and YouTube have transformed the way healing knowledge is shared, making curanderismo accessible to people across the globe. These virtual spaces, filled with videos, live sessions, and written guidance, act as digital extensions of ancestral traditions. Here, the wisdom of the abuelas meets the innovation of the digital age.

On TikTok, curandera Erika Buenaflor shares brief yet impactful videos covering traditional practices, such as performing limpias with everyday tools, interpreting the significance of ruda, and crafting teas for spiritual protection. Her content demystifies curanderismo, drawing younger audiences eager to reconnect with their cultural roots. Her relatable and engaging approach has cultivated a growing community of followers who see her videos as a bridge to ancestral wisdom.

Curanderas like Ixtoii Paloma Cervantes have embraced YouTube as a teaching platform, offering online workshops and virtual classes on curanderismo's foundational practices. Ixtoii's series includes detailed tutorials on creating altars, brewing herbal remedies, and understanding the spiritual significance of the four elements. These virtual workshops reach students from across continents, allowing curanderismo to cross borders and unite diverse communities. Through her educational content, Ixtoii ensures that the essence of curanderismo thrives in both traditional and modern contexts.

On Instagram, curandera Yadira Marie conducts live limpia ceremonies, inviting her audience to light candles, meditate, and join her in collective healing prayers. These livestreams create an intimate and sacred space, resonating with viewers from places as far away as South America and Southeast Asia. Her work demonstrates that healing is not dependent on physical proximity but thrives on shared intention and spiritual connection.

Other curanderas use social media to connect tradition with accessibility. On YouTube, practitioners share insights into everyday herbs, showing how ingredients like cinnamon and garlic—often found in kitchen pantries—can serve both spiritual and physical healing needs. Instagram becomes a place to amplify messages of empowerment through daily affirmations and videos showcasing the preparation of herbal remedies. These modern approaches remind followers that curanderismo is not distant or inaccessible—it is present in everyday life, waiting to be rediscovered.

Social media platforms also foster activism and community. Hashtags such as #DecolonizeHealing, #CuranderismoReclaimed, and #AncestralWisdom allow practitioners to share content that reclaims curanderismo's roots while resisting the commodification of spiritual practices. These movements position curanderismo not only as a healing modality but also as an act of decolonization, a way of celebrating resilience, and a means of cultural empowerment.

One of the most transformative uses of digital platforms is the creation of online healing circles. These gatherings bring participants from across time zones into shared virtual spaces, where candles are lit simultaneously, intentions are set, and prayers are spoken collectively. Such events exemplify the unifying power of curanderismo in the digital age, transcending physical separation to nurture spiritual connection.

As curanderismo moves into the digital era, its practitioners prove that tradition and technology can coexist harmoniously. Whether through livestreamed limpias, TikTok tutorials, or global healing workshops, these digital spaces ensure that the sacred work of curanderismo adapts to meet the needs of today's world.

URBAN CURANDERISMO: FINDING SACREDNESS IN CITIES

In cities where access to nature is limited, curanderas have become innovators, finding sacredness in unexpected places. Through creativity and determination, they reclaim urban spaces, transforming them into sanctuaries for healing and community. Whether on rooftops, in community gardens, or among bustling markets, these curanderas prove that the sacred exists wherever it is nurtured.

Rooftop Gardens and Green Spaces

Sofía, a curandera in New York City, transformed a rooftop into a sanctuary where healing rituals take place. Rows of lavender, basil, and mint line the edges of the rooftop, while an altar adorned with candles, stones, and small statues of saints sits at its center. "The earth's spirit is present here, even among skyscrapers," Sofía says. By day, the rooftop is a tranquil space for meditation and herbal preparation. By night, it becomes a gathering place for moonlit limpias, where participants are guided through prayers and smoke cleansings under the stars.

Sofía often incorporates elements of the urban landscape into her work. "The sound of sirens doesn't interrupt the ritual—it becomes part of it. Healing doesn't mean escaping the city; it means grounding yourself within it." One participant, a single mother named Elena, shared how attending rooftop rituals helped her reconnect with her culture while finding peace in the chaos of city life.

Sofía's space is also a teaching ground. Twice a month, she holds workshops on cultivating medicinal herbs in limited spaces, from windowsills to fire escapes. "Even in the smallest corners, plants can thrive," she says. "And where plants thrive, healing thrives."

Herbal Swaps and Community Markets

In Los Angeles, herbal swaps organized by young curanderas are revitalizing communal healing practices. These gatherings, often held in public parks or community centers, draw people from diverse backgrounds who come to trade plants like sage, rosemary, and epazote. Participants also exchange recipes for herbal remedies and share personal stories of resilience and healing.

Marisol, one of the organizers, describes these events as more than just exchanges. "Healing starts with the land but grows through community," she says. At a recent event, a participant shared how receiving a cutting of ruda from an elder reminded her of her grandmother's garden back in El Salvador. "It's not just about the herb—it's about the memories and connections it brings," she said.

Marisol also teaches attendees how to start small urban herb gardens in limited spaces, using repurposed containers like tin cans and old buckets. "You don't need a big yard to honor the earth," she explains. "Every little space you cultivate is an act of healing."

These markets are evolving into hubs for more than just herbs. Curanderas have begun offering free limpias and spiritual consultations during the events, while others sell handmade tinctures, teas, and protective amulets. The gatherings, Marisol notes, are creating a new generation of urban healers.

Revitalizing Vacant Spaces

In Chicago, curandera Leticia collaborates with urban farming collectives to grow medicinal herbs in vacant lots. These once-abandoned spaces now bloom with ruda, chamomile, and calendula, serving as both healing gardens and community hubs. "The land holds power, even when it's neglected," Leticia explains. "We're not just healing ourselves—we're healing the city."

One of her most ambitious projects transformed an empty lot near a community center into a thriving herbal garden. The space is now used for workshops on sustainable gardening, where attendees learn to grow medicinal plants like valerian and mint. Local children have also become involved, planting seeds and learning about the healing properties of the herbs. "It's not just a garden," Leticia says. "It's a place where people learn to care for the earth and each other."

These vacant spaces also become stages for rituals. On summer evenings, Leticia leads ceremonies where neighbors gather to honor the earth and set intentions for healing. She lights copal and sings traditional prayers, reminding her community that even in the heart of the city, sacredness can be found.

Urban curanderismo is more than a practice; it is a way of seeing the world. Curanderas in cities have learned to find sacredness in the everyday—from the cracks in the pavement where herbs like dandelion grow, to the breeze that carries prayers between high-rises. Through rooftop gardens, herbal swaps, and reclaimed vacant spaces, these healers transform their environments, showing that the spirit of curanderismo is not bound by geography. As Sofía reflects, "The earth is always with us, even when it looks like concrete."

THE NEXT GENERATION: BRIDGING ANCESTRAL WISDOM AND INNOVATION

The next generation of curanderas is redefining what it means to heal. They embrace their ancestral heritage while finding innovative ways to share their practices, often blending traditions with contemporary tools. Their work reflects a deep respect for their roots while addressing the unique challenges of modern communities, demonstrating that curanderismo is not static but alive, dynamic, and evolving.

Blending Cultures and Practices

In Toronto, Latina healers collaborate with First Nations communities to exchange knowledge about plant medicines and rituals tied to land stewardship. These partnerships not only preserve their respective traditions but also foster shared healing practices that honor the land they now inhabit. Rosa, a curandera who works closely with Indigenous elders, hosts seasonal ceremonies that weave together the wisdom of both cultures. In one recent event during the autumn equinox, participants gathered around a fire to offer tobacco, maize, and sage while singing songs in Nahuatl and Cree.

"Healing has no borders," Rosa explains. "Our ancestors all knew how to listen to the land. By sharing what we know, we heal the divisions created by colonization." These collaborations often include workshops where participants learn to identify local plants and their uses in both Indigenous and Latin American healing traditions. Rosa's work exemplifies how curanderismo can adapt to and integrate with new cultural landscapes while remaining true to its essence.

In another example, curandera Lucía in London has begun incorporating elements of Ayurveda into her practice after working alongside South Asian healers. "Both of our traditions see the body as part of a larger spiritual ecosystem," she says. Lucía's ceremonies now include rituals inspired by both systems, such as combining turmeric (used in Ayurvedic practices) with ruda in cleansing baths. These cross-cultural exchanges demonstrate the universality of ancestral wisdom and its potential to unite communities.

Decolonizing Healing

Younger curanderas increasingly see their work as a form of activism. Pages like @DecolonizeHealing, run by curandera Sofía, have become powerful tools for challenging the commercialization of spiritual practices and reclaiming ancestral knowledge. "Our work isn't just about remedies—it's about reclaiming what colonization tried to erase," Sofía explains. Her posts often highlight the history of curanderismo as an act of resistance, drawing parallels between past struggles and modern movements for justice.

One viral campaign launched by @DecolonizeHealing focused on the appropriation of spiritual practices. Sofía created a series of posts educating her followers on the importance of respecting cultural origins and avoiding practices stripped of their context. Her hashtag #SacredNot-Trendy sparked conversations across social media, encouraging users to reflect on the ethics of spiritual engagement.

Beyond social media, Sofía's work extends to community organizing. She recently led a workshop series titled "Healing and Resistance," which taught participants how to use curanderismo practices like limpias and protective bundles as tools for empowerment during protests and social justice movements. "Healing isn't passive," she says. "It's about fortifying ourselves so we can show up for our communities."

Empowering Marginalized Communities

In Oakland, Leticia runs a wellness collective that offers free workshops on herbal medicine, spiritual healing, and sustainable gardening. Her sessions are designed to address systemic issues like food deserts, environmental degradation, and trauma in underserved communities. "Healing isn't just personal—it's political," she says. "We heal ourselves so we can fight for change."

At one recent workshop, Leticia guided participants in creating healing salves using locally foraged plants like plantain and yarrow. Many attendees had never considered their neighborhood greenery as a resource for healing. "Our neighborhoods might feel abandoned, but the earth still provides for us," Leticia told them. Her collective also organizes monthly "healing circles" in community gardens, where participants share their struggles, offer prayers, and leave with herbal remedies.

Leticia's work goes beyond individual healing. She collaborates with local activists to address structural issues, such as lobbying for urban farming initiatives and equitable access to green spaces. "Healing the land and healing the people are inseparable," she says. Her wellness collective has become a beacon of hope in Oakland, illustrating how curanderismo can drive social transformation.

The next generation of curanderas not only carries forward the traditions of their ancestors but also reimagines them for the future. Whether through blending cultures, challenging systems of oppression, or empowering their communities, these healers prove that curanderismo is a practice of both preservation and revolution. By addressing modern challenges while honoring ancestral wisdom, they ensure that curanderismo remains a vital force in a changing world.

STORIES OF RESILIENCE: TESTIMONIOS OF MODERN CURANDERAS

The stories of modern curanderas are threads in a larger tapestry of resilience, adaptation, and cultural preservation. Each testimony is a reminder that curanderismo is not bound by geography or time—it evolves to meet the needs of those who carry it forward. These curanderas, navigating the complexities of the modern world, prove that healing remains a sacred act of resistance and renewal.

Testimonio of Clara in London

Clara, a college student in London, began exploring curanderismo after years of feeling disconnected from her Mexican roots. Raised in a family that had migrated to England when she was a child, Clara grew up surrounded by stories of her abuela's healing rituals but had little direct experience with them. "I didn't grow up with these traditions, but they've always been in my blood," she says.

Her journey began during a particularly challenging time in her life, when the pressures of school and of living far from her family began to take a toll on her mental health. In search of grounding, Clara started lighting candles and brewing herbal teas—simple rituals that reminded her of her grandmother's prayers. Over time, her curiosity deepened, and she began researching the plants and prayers her abuela had used.

Today, Clara runs an online platform called Raíces Vivas (Living Roots), where she documents her journey and shares what she learns about curanderismo. Her posts range from recipes for herbal remedies to reflections on cultural identity. One of her most popular videos, titled "Healing Through Ancestry," features Clara preparing a limpia using rosemary and lavender while explaining the spiritual significance of each step. "Curanderismo gave me back a part of myself I didn't know was missing," she says. Through her platform, Clara has connected with followers from across the globe, many of whom share similar stories of reconnecting with ancestral practices.

Testimonio of María in Los Angeles

María Luz, a curandera based in Los Angeles, blends tradition with technology to reach a global audience. Every week, she streams live virtual ceremonies from her home altar, inviting participants to join her in prayers, meditations, and limpias. Her altar, adorned with candles, photos of her ancestors, and bundles of sage and ruda, serves as a focal point for her work.

María Luz offers an innovative fusion of ancestral and digital healing practices. Her ability to adapt rituals for livestreams demonstrates the resilience and modernization of curanderismo. One of her regular viewers, a migrant worker in Texas, shared how these ceremonies helped her feel connected to her homeland despite years of separation. "It's a way of carrying our roots wherever we go," María explains. For many participants, her livestreams are more than just rituals—they are acts of communal healing, where people separated by distance come together to honor their shared heritage.

María's work extends beyond virtual ceremonies. She also offers one-on-one distance healings, during which she performs a limpia while the recipient participates from their own space. In one session, María guided a young woman experiencing grief through a cleansing ritual using an egg, instructing her to hold the egg while María whispered prayers. "Healing isn't confined to proximity," she says. "It's about intention and connection." Her ability to adapt traditional practices to modern tools ensures that curanderismo remains accessible to those who need it most.

Testimonio of Alejandro in Miami

Alejandro, one of a growing number of male curanderos, practices in Miami, where he combines curanderismo with community activism. Born into a family of healers in Veracruz, Alejandro learned the basics of herbal remedies and prayer from his mother. However, it wasn't until he immigrated to the United States and saw the struggles of his community that he decided to fully embrace his calling.

"Curanderismo isn't just about physical healing," Alejandro explains. "It's about restoring balance to the soul and the community." In Miami, he works with migrant families, offering free limpias and herbal remedies at local community centers. One of his most impactful projects is a youth mentorship program that teaches teenagers how to identify and use local plants for healing. "I want them to know that they carry their ancestors' wisdom, even if they're far from home," he says.

Alejandro's ceremonies often incorporate elements of storytelling, with participants encouraged to share their struggles and triumphs. One participant, a teenager navigating the challenges of undocumented life, described how Alejandro's rituals gave her the courage to embrace her identity. "He helped me see that my heritage is my strength," she says.

Testimonio of Esperanza in Chicago

Esperanza, a third-generation curandera in Chicago, combines her family's traditional practices with a focus on mental health. "Our ancestors didn't call it anxiety or depression," she says, "but they knew how to heal the spirit." Through her practice, Esperanza integrates curanderismo with mindfulness techniques, helping clients navigate the pressures of modern life.

In her neighborhood, which is home to a large Mexican American population, Esperanza offers group healing sessions at a local library. These sessions, titled "Healing in the City," are designed to reconnect participants with their ancestral roots. "Even in a city as busy as Chicago, the earth is still with us," she reminds her clients. Her work has drawn attention for its holistic approach, blending herbal remedies with guided meditations and journaling exercises.

One of her most memorable sessions involved a woman struggling with generational trauma. Through a series of rituals, including a limpia and a reflective journaling exercise, the woman found clarity and a renewed sense of purpose. "Esperanza didn't just help me heal," the woman says. "She helped me see the strength in my story."

The modern curandera is a testament to the resilience and adaptability of curanderismo. Whether through online platforms, urban rituals, or cross-cultural exchanges, these healers honor the past while embracing the present. Their stories remind us that healing is not static—it is an evolving dialogue between tradition and innovation, rooted in the sacred yet open to change. By reaching hearts and souls across the globe, these curanderas ensure that the wisdom of curanderismo continues to thrive in every corner of the world.

THE SACRED AND THE EVOLVING

Somos las curanderas del mañana,
hijas de las estrellas y del barro,
caminamos entre las sombras de las ciudades
y los ecos de los volcanes,
curando al mundo, un alma a la vez.
We are the curanderas of tomorrow,
daughters of the stars and the clay,
walking between the shadows of cities
and the echoes of volcanoes,
healing the world, one soul at a time.

Llevamos en nuestras manos las cicatrices del tiempo,
y en nuestras palabras, los cantos de los ancestros.
Nuestros rezos son ríos que atraviesan fronteras,
creando puentes donde otros ven abismos.
We carry in our hands the scars of time,
and in our words, the songs of the ancestors.
Our prayers are rivers that cross borders,
creating bridges where others see chasms.

Aquí, entre el concreto y la pantalla,
la tierra aún nos llama por nuestro nombre,
y aunque el mundo nos quiera olvidar,
en cada hierba que crece, renacemos.
Here, between the concrete and the screen,
the earth still calls us by name,
and though the world may try to forget us,
in every herb that grows, we are reborn.

No somos espectros del pasado;
somos fuego que nunca se apaga,
el rayo que divide la tormenta,
la semilla que rompe el asfalto.
We are not ghosts of the past;

we are fire that never fades,
the lightning that splits the storm,
the seed that breaks through asphalt.

Nuestra medicina es el aliento de las montañas,
el sabor del agua que recuerda el océano,
y el susurro del viento que atraviesa generaciones.
Our medicine is the breath of mountains,
the taste of water that remembers the ocean,
and the whisper of wind that crosses generations.

Con cada ritual encendemos la memoria,
una vela para los que perdimos,
una oración para los que vendrán
y un grito para los que resisten.
With every ritual, we ignite memory,
a candle for those we lost,
a prayer for those to come,
and a cry for those who resist.

No somos ramas separadas;
somos un solo árbol,
creciendo hacia el infinito,
alimentado por raíces que nadie puede cortar.
We are not separate branches;
we are one tree,
growing toward the infinite,
fed by roots no one can sever.

• • •

We celebrate the timeless essence of the curandera, a healer who walks confidently between worlds. This poem speaks to the resilience of curanderismo as it adapts to modern challenges while remaining deeply rooted in ancestral wisdom. In each act of healing, whether through the digital airwaves or among the cracks of a bustling city, curanderas carry the sacred forward. They are both guardians of tradition and architects of evolution, proving that the spirit of healing is eternal and unbound by time or place. As the world shifts and grows, so too does the curandera's role, always grounded in her unshakable connection to Madre Tierra and the people she serves.

The modern curandera reminds us that healing is not a relic of the past but a living, evolving force. It bridges generations, cultures, and worlds, teaching us that resilience and sacredness can thrive anywhere—be it in the wild fields of ancestral lands or the cracks of a bustling city sidewalk. In a world that often feels fragmented, the curandera offers wholeness. Her work calls each of us to reconnect—with our roots, our communities, and the earth itself. Her tools may vary, from ruda to livestreams, but her message remains the same: healing begins with intention, and it is a shared journey.

As you close this chapter, consider the role of healing in your own life. How can you honor the wisdom of those who came before you? How can you nurture your connection to the sacred, wherever you are? And most importantly, how can you carry the spirit of curanderismo forward—through small rituals, acts of care, or the simple act of remembering? The curandera's light is not hers alone—it is a flame passed from generation to generation, inviting us all to become stewards of healing and transformation. May her wisdom guide you to rediscover the sacred in yourself and the world around you.

The inclusive practices of modern curanderas naturally intersect with the reclamation of historically erased and marginalized roles. In particular, queer and gender-diverse healers are redefining what it means to be a curandera, reclaiming spaces of healing once denied to them. Chapter 8 explores the queering of curanderismo, celebrating the voices and rituals of these transformative practitioners.

CHAPTER 8

QUEERING CURANDERISMO

OPENING INVOCATION

Te llamo desde los márgenes,
donde la sombra se convierte en luz
y las heridas florecen como jacarandas en primavera.
I call to you from the margins,
where shadow becomes light
and wounds bloom like jacarandas in spring.

Somos hijes del agua y el fuego,
del barro que no conoce moldes,
y de los ecos que se niegan a morir.
We are children of water and fire,
of clay that knows no molds,
and of echoes that refuse to die.

Aquí, entre caminos cruzados y cuerpos sagrados,
el corazón se abre como maguey bajo el sol,
ofreciendo su néctar sin temor.
Here, between crossed paths and sacred bodies,

the heart opens like maguey under the sun,
offering its nectar without fear.

No somos rotos; somos completos.
No somos invisibles; somos reflejos de estrellas,
brillando en un mundo que necesita recordar.
We are not broken; we are whole.
We are not invisible; we are reflections of stars,
shining in a world that needs to remember.

Te llamamos, Madre Tierra,
porque incluso en la negación,
tu voz nos encuentra, siempre susurrando:
"Ustedes también son míos."
We call to you, Mother Earth,
because even in denial,
your voice finds us, always whispering:
"You are mine too."

• • •

The invocation sets the tone for a chapter dedicated to embracing the fluidity and expansiveness of healing traditions. It calls us to recognize that the sacred is not confined by societal constructs or binaries—it thrives in the liminal spaces where identities intersect, grow, and resist. Queer curanderismo reminds us that to heal is to honor the full spectrum of existence, acknowledging the beauty in diversity and the strength in unity. These practices challenge us to expand our understanding of what it means to belong, teaching that healing is not a privilege but an inherent right. Just as the earth nurtures all who walk upon it, curanderismo evolves to embrace every soul who seeks its wisdom, making space for those who have often been silenced or overlooked.

Curanderismo has always thrived in liminal spaces—between the sacred and the everyday, the earthly and the divine. It is no surprise, then, that it has become a source of healing and empowerment for LGBTQ+ communities, whose identities often inhabit the margins of tradition and society. From its precolonial roots, where gender-fluid shamans were revered as bridges to the spirit world, to its modern resurgence among queer curanderas and curanderos reclaiming ancestral practices, curanderismo continues to evolve as a practice of radical inclusion and transformation.

This chapter explores how LGBTQ+ practitioners are redefining curanderismo to honor their identities while addressing the unique wounds and strengths of queer communities. Through testimonios, rituals, and cross-cultural collaborations, these healers remind us that the sacred belongs to all, regardless of gender, sexuality, or societal expectation.

As curanderismo evolves to embrace these diverse identities, the language used to describe its practitioners also shifts to reflect this inclusivity. Language has always been a tool of both colonization and resistance, and within curanderismo, it continues to adapt to the needs of the community.

The evolution of curanderismo naturally invites an evolution of language. Historically, the terms *curandero* (masculine) and *curandera* (feminine) have been used to describe practitioners of this sacred tradition. However, as contemporary healers expand the boundaries of identity, these terms may not fully encompass the diversity of those who carry the practice forward. In response, the term *curandere* emerges as a gender-neutral alternative, honoring both tradition and the fluidity of modern identities. *Curandere* reflects the practice's deep roots in collective healing while embracing a framework of inclusivity. It challenges colonial frameworks that imposed binary gender constructs, offering a term that resonates with decolonial and intersectional perspectives. By centering relationality and community rather than individual roles tied to gender, *curandere* invites us to reimagine the healer's role as a shared, fluid, and expansive identity.

This term is not merely a linguistic innovation—it is a reclamation. It speaks to the adaptability of curanderismo as it navigates contemporary realities, from queerness to diasporic resilience, without severing ties to its ancestral wisdom. *Curandere* becomes a symbol of healing that transcends boundaries—whether they are cultural, spiritual, or gendered—and offers a vision of curanderismo that is as inclusive as it is transformative. This shift toward inclusivity in language, embodied in terms like *curandere*, is not a departure from tradition but a return to the fluidity of spirit that has always been present in curanderismo. By reclaiming ancestral roots while embracing modern understandings of identity, curanderismo demonstrates its ability to transcend boundaries of all kinds.

ANCESTRAL ROOTS AND THE FLUIDITY OF SPIRIT

Before colonization, many Indigenous cultures across the Americas recognized gender as fluid and expansive, a reflection of the natural world's complexity and balance. Gender-diverse individuals, often referred to as Two-Spirit in some Indigenous North American traditions, were revered as healers, mediators, and spiritual guides. These roles were not peripheral but central to the community's spiritual and social fabric, seen as bridging the earthly and the divine.

The Nahua concept of macehuales—those who embodied the duality of existence—was one such example. In Nahua cosmology, duality was fundamental to understanding the universe, with masculine and feminine energies complementing rather than opposing each other. Those who carried both were believed to channel harmony, acting as intermediaries between the human and the sacred. Similarly, the Maya ajq'ijab (daykeepers) often included individuals who defied conventional gender roles. These healers were entrusted with maintaining balance within the community, consulting sacred calendars, performing rituals, and interpreting dreams to guide collective decisions.

In *Gender Trouble: Feminism and the Subversion of Identity*, queer theorist Judith Butler argues that gender is not a fixed category but a series of repeated acts that create the illusion of stability. This perspective resonates with Indigenous understandings of gender as fluid and relational, rather than binary and static. In "Heterosexualism and the Colonial/Modern Gender System," María Lugones extends this analysis by situating gender binaries as a colonial imposition, arguing that precolonial societies often recognized multiple genders as integral to community and spiritual life. The Nahua and Maya traditions of gender-diverse healers exemplify this fluidity, illustrating that these roles were not anomalies but central to maintaining balance and harmony within their cosmologies.

In Andean traditions, chachawarmi—a concept encapsulating the duality of masculine and feminine—extended beyond individuals to define how societies functioned in balance. People who existed beyond these binaries were not anomalies but vital contributors to sustaining this equilibrium. Their unique perspectives were considered gifts, allowing them to navigate and mediate between different realms of existence.

Colonial forces disrupted these traditions through systemic violence and the imposition of rigid gender binaries. The Spanish Inquisition, for example, targeted gender-diverse individuals, labeling them heretics and witches, while Catholic missionaries sought to erase Indigenous beliefs by replacing them with patriarchal structures. This erasure extended to the demonization of healers and the suppression of sacred practices that celebrated fluidity.

Despite centuries of colonial oppression, the spirit of gender expansiveness survived, encoded in rituals, oral histories, and healing practices passed down through generations. Many communities continued to honor gender-nonconforming healers in secret, integrating their wisdom into the broader curanderismo tradition. Queer curanderes today are part of this lineage, reclaiming ancestral roles as sacred mediators and healers.

Gloria Anzaldúa's concept of the borderlands—both physical and metaphorical—provides a framework for understanding the work of queer curanderes as acts of decolonization. By existing in the liminal spaces between tradition and innovation, these practitioners challenge colonial erasure and reclaim spiritual roles that honor gender expansiveness. Similarly, Linda Tuhiwai Smith's *Decolonizing Methodologies* underscores the importance of recovering Indigenous epistemologies, a process mirrored in the rituals and narratives of queer curanderismo. These healers not only preserve ancestral knowledge but actively transform it to reflect the needs of modern communities, embodying what Anzaldúa called "new mestiza consciousness."

For modern queer practitioners, this reclamation is both deeply personal and profoundly political. It challenges the colonial narrative that sought to erase their identities and reaffirms the sacredness of their existence. When a curandere lights a candle or prepares a limpia, they are not only performing a ritual but also resisting the forces that have long sought to silence them. Their work becomes an act of healing not only for the self but for the generations that came before them, whose voices echo through these sacred acts.

This resurgence of fluidity within curanderismo reflects a broader movement of decolonization, where Indigenous and queer identities are celebrated as integral to the healing process. By honoring these ancestral roots, curanderes embody a profound truth: the sacred cannot be confined to binaries or borders—it exists wherever authenticity and spirit meet.

Rather than solely framing queer curandere practices through Butler's theory of performativity, this chapter turns to María Lugones's theory of the colonial/modern gender system and José Esteban Muñoz's concept of disidentification to understand how queer and trans curanderes survive, and how they subvert and regenerate healing practices, within racialized and colonial systems.

MODERN QUEER CURANDERAS AND THEIR PRACTICES

Today's queer curanderas, curanderos, and curanderes embody the transformative essence of curanderismo, blending traditional practices with symbols of resilience, identity, and activism. By embracing fluidity and inclusivity, they redefine healing as an act that transcends binaries and creates space for belonging and empowerment. Rooted in traditional practices yet transformed by the unique experiences of LGBTQ+ individuals, their work redefines curanderismo as a living, adaptive force. These healers honor their ancestors while forging new paths, addressing the specific wounds of queer communities—shame, marginalization, and disconnection—through rituals that center empowerment and belonging.

For queer curanderes, their practice often begins with addressing the intersections of identity. Many LGBTQ+ individuals carry the weight of internalized oppression, feeling alienated not only from dominant society but also from ancestral traditions that have historically excluded or erased them. Modern queer healers recognize this pain and transform it into a source of strength. They draw from the deep well of curanderismo's wisdom, blending its teachings with symbols, rituals, and language that affirm the diversity and resilience of queer lives.

Kimberlé Crenshaw's theory of intersectionality underscores the importance of recognizing how overlapping identities shape experiences of oppression and resilience. For queer curanderes, this perspective is essential in designing healing practices that address not just queerness but also the compounded challenges of racism, classism, and xenophobia. For instance, curanderas working with undocumented LGBTQ+

clients often incorporate elements of protection against xenophobic harm alongside rituals affirming queer identity. Luz, a nonbinary curandera in Austin, integrates lavender and basil into her limpias for migrant clients, explaining, "Lavender brings peace to turbulent journeys, while basil offers protection against those who wish to harm us." By centering intersectionality, these healers challenge the reductive frameworks that pathologize queer communities, emphasizing instead their capacity for resilience and holistic healing.

Testimonio of Sofía (They/Them)

Sofía, a nonbinary curandera based in San Francisco, describes their practice as "healing at the intersections." For them, curanderismo is not simply a return to tradition but a reimagining of it, one that embraces the complexity of queer identity. Their limpias often incorporate symbols of queer resilience, such as rainbow-colored candles, altarpieces representing chosen family, and even flags from LGBTQ+ movements.

"Curanderismo taught me that we are all connected to the earth," they say. "As queer people, we often feel disconnected—from our families, our ancestors, and even ourselves. But this practice reminds us that we are whole, that we've always been part of something sacred."

Sofía's most popular ritual, the limpia de identidad, is specifically designed to help clients release internalized shame and reconnect with their authentic selves. Using ruda for protection, lavender for peace, and rosemary to symbolize memory and self-awareness, the ritual is deeply transformative. "The plants do more than cleanse," Sofía explains. "They remind us of who we are. They whisper to us that we are enough." Their ceremonies often include elements that blend the ancient and the contemporary. Poetry and music play central roles, with Sofía combining precolonial Nahua chants with modern queer anthems. One of their clients, a trans man navigating a painful estrangement from his family, described the experience as "a reminder that I'm still loved, still connected—even when the world tells me otherwise."

Innovations in Ritual and Practice

Modern queer curanderes are also innovating their practices to reflect the diversity of their clients and the changing world around them. Their rituals often include elements that acknowledge chosen family, intersectionality, and community care—concepts deeply embedded in queer culture.

Intersectional analysis, which examines how overlapping identities create unique experiences of oppression, is central to understanding the work of queer curanderes. These healers address not only the traumas of queerness but also the compounded effects of race, ethnicity, class, and migration. One of the healing paths explored in this book is a transitional identity-centered ritual shaped within community-based and elemental healing practices. This ceremony, known as the "Embracing the Becoming" ritual, is a life-transition rite that invites embodiment, the elements, and community witness to guide transformation. It is an intentional process of honoring identity as a sacred evolution, not as pathology. Rituals like the "Embracing the Becoming" ceremony for trans clients reflect this intersectional approach, acknowledging the multifaceted nature of identity while creating a sacred container for healing. By centering the whole person in their practice, curanderes challenge the reductive frameworks that have historically pathologized their communities. For example, curandere Alex in New York City incorporates "altars of resistance" into their healing sessions. These altars feature objects that symbolize the resilience of LGBTQ+ communities, such as photographs of activists like Marsha P. Johnson and Sylvia Rivera, alongside traditional curanderismo tools like copal and crystals. Alex explains, "Our activism is sacred, and our rituals honor those who fought for us to exist. Healing isn't just personal—it's collective."

Similarly, some queer curanderes incorporate body-positive practices into their limpias, addressing the shame and dysphoria that many LGBTQ+ individuals experience. For Luz in Austin, their limpias include affirmations spoken aloud while the client holds a mirror. "It's not enough to cleanse away the pain," Luz says. "We have to fill that space with love and affirmation. That's where the real healing begins."

Testimonio of Mateo (He/They)

Mateo, a queer curandero in Los Angeles, describes their work as "a rebellion against forgetting." As a child of immigrants, Mateo grew up feeling disconnected from his family's traditions but found his way back to curanderismo as a young adult. Now he uses his practice to bridge generational and cultural divides within queer Latinx communities.

One of Mateo's signature rituals is the limpia de amor propio (self-love cleansing), designed specifically for LGBTQ+ individuals struggling with self-acceptance. Using a blend of roses for love, sage for clarity, and orange blossoms for joy, Mateo guides clients through a process of releasing shame and embracing their beauty. "Our ancestors fought to keep this knowledge alive," Mateo says. "And I believe they fought for all of us—not just the parts of us that fit neatly into tradition."

Mateo also incorporates elements of storytelling into their work, encouraging clients to share their own journeys as part of the healing process. "Stories are sacred," he says. "When we share them, we reclaim the power that shame tried to steal from us."

HEALING AS RECLAMATION AND RESISTANCE

For queer curanderes, healing is not just about addressing personal wounds—it is a radical act of reclamation. By reclaiming curanderismo as a space for queer identity, these healers challenge the colonial and patriarchal narratives that sought to erase them. Their work is deeply political, creating spaces where LGBTQ+ individuals can not only heal but also thrive.

Queer curanderismo draws strength from intersectional theories that illuminate the layered experiences of oppression and resilience within LGBTQ+ communities. Queer curanderes embody this intersectional approach by crafting rituals that address the compounded traumas of racism, homophobia, transphobia, and colonialism. A limpia for a queer immigrant, for instance, might include elements that honor migration journeys—such as crossing sacred thresholds—and affirm their place in their chosen community. Similarly, rituals like Mateo's limpia de amor propio acknowledge the intersections of cultural disconnection and queer identity, offering clients a path toward reclaiming their stories as sources of power. By weaving intersectionality into their practices, queer curanderes not only heal individuals but also affirm the interconnectedness of personal and collective liberation.

Intergenerational healing plays a vital role in queer curanderismo, bridging the past with the future to restore a continuum often fractured by colonialism, migration, and systemic oppression. Through their practices, queer curanderes honor the wisdom of their ancestors while creating pathways for younger generations to reclaim and reinterpret this knowledge. Rituals like the limpia del nombre not only affirm individual identity but also reconnect clients to the names, prayers, and stories of those who came before them. By invoking ancestral guidance and integrating contemporary symbols of resilience, these healers emphasize that queer existence is not a break from tradition but a continuation of it. This approach counters narratives of disconnection, demonstrating that healing is both a personal and collective process, rooted in shared histories and carried forward in acts of resistance and love.

In these spaces, the boundaries between healer and community often dissolve. Healing becomes a collective endeavor, where clients are encouraged to participate actively in their own rituals and to bring the teachings of curanderismo into their daily lives. Whether through a shared altar, a communal limpia, or a gathering of stories, queer curanderes demonstrate that healing is strongest when it is rooted in connection. As Sofía reflects, "Queer people have always been healers. We've always found ways to survive, to protect each other, to create beauty out of pain. Curanderismo is just one way we remember that—and one way we make sure the next generation remembers, too."

Queer curanderismo, while rooted in personal and collective healing, also demands accountability to the communities it serves. Practitioners must navigate the complexities of representing intersecting identities, ensuring that their work honors both ancestral traditions and the lived experiences of LGBTQ+ individuals. This includes addressing the risk of cultural commodification, especially in spaces where curanderismo intersects with online visibility and commercial platforms. Queer curanderes like Sofía and Mateo emphasize the importance of giving back to the communities that shaped their practices, offering sliding-scale or donation-based services and prioritizing those who face systemic barriers to accessing care. Accountability also extends to how rituals and stories are shared—ensuring that cultural practices are contextualized and that sacred knowledge is not reduced to trends. By grounding their work in principles of consent, reciprocity, and transparency, queer curanderes reaffirm their role as stewards of both tradition and transformation, creating spaces where healing is inclusive, ethical, and deeply rooted in respect.

QUEERING RITUALS AND CREATING INCLUSIVE SPACES

Queer curanderes are transforming the practice of curanderismo by creating rituals that honor the diversity and complexity of LGBTQ+ identities. These rituals are not only acts of personal healing but also celebrations of queer resilience, community, and love. By blending traditional practices with modern adaptations, queer healers create spaces where their communities feel seen, affirmed, and empowered. These rituals often address the unique challenges faced by LGBTQ+ individuals, such as estrangement from biological families, societal marginalization, and the search for belonging.

Queer Healing Circles: A Safe Haven in Los Angeles

In Los Angeles, community healer Alex hosts monthly "Queer Healing Circles," where participants gather to share in the transformative power of collective healing. These events are held in a backyard sanctuary filled with vibrant plants, candles, and a central altar adorned with offerings of fruit, flowers, and symbolic objects. The gatherings begin with a group limpia, in which participants pass bundles of sage and rosemary, wafting smoke over each other while Alex chants prayers for protection and self-acceptance.

The heart of the circle lies in collective altar-building, a practice Alex describes as "a way to reclaim sacredness in the stories we tell about ourselves." Participants are invited to bring objects that symbolize their journey—photos of loved ones, small heirlooms, or items that represent personal struggles or triumphs. Together, they construct an altar that becomes a living testament to the strength and diversity of their community.

One participant, a nonbinary artist named Jaime, describes the circles as "a place where I can bring my whole self, where my identity isn't just accepted—it's celebrated." For many attendees, these gatherings are a rare opportunity to connect with others who understand the intersections of queerness and spirituality, offering a sense of solidarity that extends far beyond the circle itself.

Queer curanderismo reflects the richness of regional and cultural diversity, with practices adapting to the unique landscapes and histories of various locales. In New Mexico, curandero Marco incorporates desert flora such as sagebrush and ocotillo into limpias, blending local plant medicine with prayers rooted in trans and queer resilience. Meanwhile, in Chicago, curandera Esperanza weaves the history of Mexican migration into her altars, adding objects like miniature trains and symbolic keys to represent journeys and new beginnings. These adaptations demonstrate that queer curanderismo is not monolithic but deeply connected to the places and people it serves. By honoring the specific cultural and environmental contexts of their communities, queer healers ensure that curanderismo remains a living tradition, shaped by the needs and strengths of each region.

Ritual Example: The Altar of Chosen Family

In queer communities, chosen family often plays a vital role, filling the void left by strained or severed relationships with biological relatives. Queer curanderes honor this reality by creating altars dedicated to chosen family, recognizing these bonds as sacred and deserving of reverence.

An altar of chosen family is built with intention and love, incorporating photographs of chosen family members, meaningful objects like letters or gifts exchanged, and items that represent shared memories. Candles are lit for each person represented, their flames symbolizing the light these individuals bring into one another's lives. At the center of the altar, curanderes often place a symbolic object—a bowl of water for cleansing and renewal, a cluster of crystals for strength, or a bundle of herbs for protection.

The ritual surrounding the altar includes a moment of reflection, in which participants express gratitude for the love and support they have received. This may be followed by a prayer or invocation, such as:

> Por los que nos han elegido,
> por los que nos han amado como somos,
> y por los que han sido nuestra fortaleza en los momentos oscuros.
> For those who have chosen us,
> for those who have loved us as we are,
> and for those who have been our strength in dark moments.

For queer individuals navigating the complexities of family estrangement or rejection, this ritual becomes a powerful act of healing. It acknowledges the pain of loss while celebrating the resilience found in chosen connections.

Inclusive Spaces for Grief and Celebration

Queer curanderes also design rituals to address the collective grief and joy of their communities. In times of loss, such as the passing of a loved one or the anniversary of historical tragedies like the Pulse nightclub shooting, curanderes create ceremonies to honor the departed while holding space for collective mourning.

For example, a curandera named Eli in San Diego leads annual remembrance ceremonies during Pride Month, combining elements of curanderismo with modern queer symbolism. Participants are invited to write the names of loved ones they wish to honor on pieces of paper, which are then burned in a communal fire as a symbol of transformation and release. "Grief can be heavy," Eli says, "but when we share it, we find strength in each other."

These ceremonies also serve as spaces for celebration, blending mourning with the joy of queer existence. Drumming, singing, and dancing are often incorporated, reminding participants that even in the face of loss, their community is vibrant, resilient, and alive.

Queering Rituals: From Tradition to Innovation

Queer curanderes approach their work with a spirit of innovation, adapting traditional practices to reflect the lived realities of LGBTQ+ individuals. For some, this involves creating rituals that address specific experiences, such as healing from religious trauma or embracing gender transitions.

Curandera Luz in Austin, for example, offers a ritual called "Embracing the Becoming," designed for trans and nonbinary individuals undergoing gender affirmation. The ritual includes a symbolic shedding of old identities, represented by burning pieces of paper with words that no longer resonate, followed by a blessing with lavender-infused water to welcome the new. "It's a way of saying goodbye to what no longer serves us and stepping fully into our truth," Luz explains.

Another curandera, Christian in Miami, incorporates elements of queer activism into their practice. During a limpia, Christian often asks clients to visualize their healing not just as something that affects themselves but as a ripple effect that strengthens their community. "When we heal, we empower," Christian says. "And when we empower, we create a future where we can all thrive."

Expanding Sacredness

Through their rituals and spaces, queer curanderes affirm that healing is not a one-size-fits-all process. Their work challenges traditional notions of who is allowed to hold sacred roles, reminding us that curanderismo has always been a practice of inclusion, adaptability, and resilience. By honoring chosen family, creating space for grief and celebration, and adapting rituals to meet the needs of their communities, these healers demonstrate that the sacred belongs to everyone—no matter their gender, sexuality, or path. In their hands, curanderismo continues to evolve, carrying forward its essence while embracing new dimensions of love and connection.

ACTIVISM AND DECOLONIZATION THROUGH QUEER CURANDERISMO

For many queer curanderes, their work exists at the intersection of healing and activism. Curanderismo has always been a practice of resistance—born from the survival strategies of Indigenous communities during colonial violence—and queer practitioners continue this legacy by addressing the systemic oppressions their communities face today. Their healing rituals, workshops, and public platforms challenge homophobia, transphobia, and the lingering effects of colonialism, reclaiming curanderismo as a space for liberation and empowerment.

In a world that often seeks to commodify spirituality or exclude marginalized voices, queer curanderes embody a radical act of decolonization. They assert that healing is not apolitical; it is deeply intertwined with identity, history, and community. By incorporating queer narratives into curanderismo, they resist the erasure of their ancestors' traditions while redefining those traditions to reflect the modern struggles and strengths of LGBTQ+ people.

Social Media as an Activist Tool

Social media platforms have become powerful tools for queer curanderes to share their knowledge, organize movements, and connect with a global community. Hashtags like #QueerCuranderismo, #DecolonizeHealing, and #AncestralWisdom create digital spaces where healers and seekers can find each other, exchange ideas, and amplify marginalized voices.

Curandera Sofía, who runs the Instagram page @SacredQueerRoots, posts daily affirmations and guides to ancestral practices. Her posts range from step-by-step instructions for preparing herbal remedies to reflections on healing from generational trauma. One of her viral campaigns, titled "Sacred Not Trendy," critiques the commercialization of curanderismo while advocating for its decolonized practice. Sofía explains, "Our traditions are sacred acts of survival. They're not trends to be sold or stripped of their context."

In addition to education, queer curanderas use social media to organize collective rituals and raise awareness about social justice issues. During Trans Day of Remembrance, a collective of queer curanderes in Texas hosted a virtual candlelight vigil streamed on multiple platforms. Participants were guided through a meditation, a prayer for the lives lost, and a collective intention-setting ritual to advocate for trans rights. This event, attended by hundreds across the globe, exemplifies how digital activism can blend with spiritual practice to create meaningful change.

Testimonio of Marco (He/Him)

Marco, a trans curandero based in New Mexico, is a healer and activist whose work centers on supporting trans and nonbinary youth. His practice often begins with rituals designed to affirm his clients' sense of belonging and sacredness. "Healing is political," Marco asserts. "When I guide a young person through a limpia, I'm not just cleansing them—I'm showing them that they belong, that their existence is sacred."

One of Marco's most impactful rituals is the limpia del nombre, a ritual for trans individuals who are affirming a new name. During this ceremony, Marco prepares a sacred space with flowers, candles, and herbs like rosemary and basil. He invites the client to speak their chosen name aloud for the first time while he offers prayers for protection and clarity. "It's about giving them a moment to be fully seen and celebrated," he says. Clients often describe the ritual as transformative, helping them feel grounded in their identity and connected to their ancestors.

Marco's activism extends beyond individual healing. He organizes workshops on ancestral healing practices for LGBTQ+ communities, blending education with empowerment. These workshops, titled "Reclaiming Our Sacredness," teach participants how to use plants, prayers, and rituals to address personal and collective trauma. Marco views this work as essential to creating spaces where trans and queer individuals can find healing outside of systems that often pathologize or exclude them. "Colonialism tried to erase us," he says, "but through curanderismo, we can remember who we are and where we come from."

Ritual as Resistance

For queer curanderas, rituals are acts of resistance that challenge colonial narratives and celebrate the inherent sacredness of LGBTQ+ identities. One such example is the Queer Liberation Altar, created by curandere Alex in Los Angeles during Pride Month. The altar incorporates symbols of resistance, including photographs of queer activists, rainbow candles, and herbs like ruda and sage for protection. During the ceremony, participants are invited to offer prayers for their community and to write down their fears or struggles on slips of paper, which are then burned in a ritual fire. "Every prayer is a spark," Alex says. "Together, they light the way forward."

Judith Butler's concept of performativity provides a lens for understanding queer rituals as acts that both reveal and resist the constraints of imposed identities. Rituals like the Queer Liberation Altar are performative not in the sense of being artificial, but in their ability to create new realities through repeated symbolic acts. By lighting candles for activists or burning fears in ritual fires, queer curanderes transform moments of individual vulnerability into collective resistance, affirming their communities' right to exist and thrive.

Another example comes from curandera Luz, who leads "Healing the Colonial Wound" workshops in Austin. These sessions combine traditional limpia rituals with discussions about the historical erasure of queer and Indigenous identities. Participants are encouraged to reflect on how colonialism has shaped their experiences and to use curanderismo as a tool for reclaiming their narratives. "When we heal ourselves, we heal the stories that have been silenced," Luz explains.

José Esteban Muñoz's concept of "queer futurity"—the idea of imagining a world not yet realized but deeply desired—illuminates the transformative power of rituals like the limpia de identidad and limpia de amor propio. These ceremonies are more than acts of self-care; they are radical reimaginings of identity that resist societal erasure. By guiding clients to release internalized shame and embrace their authentic selves, queer curanderes create a spiritual space where new possibilities for belonging and self-worth can emerge. These rituals exemplify Muñoz's assertion that queerness is always oriented toward hope and a better future.

Queer theoretical frameworks deepen the understanding of modern queer curanderismo by situating it within broader discourses of identity, resistance, and belonging. Judith Butler's concept of performativity underscores how rituals such as the limpia de identidad do more than affirm the self—they actively reshape the ways queer individuals navigate and resist imposed norms. These rituals, through repeated symbolic acts, create new realities that affirm queer existence as sacred and integral. Similarly, Gloria Anzaldúa's theory of the borderlands speaks directly to the work of queer curanderes who inhabit the intersections of gender, sexuality, and spirituality. By drawing from these frameworks, queer curanderismo is positioned not just as a practice of healing but as a radical reimagining of what it means to thrive within and beyond the margins of society.

Queering Decolonization: Reclaiming the Sacred

Queering curanderismo is not about changing its essence but expanding its reach. LGBTQ+ practitioners bring their identities into the sacred space, not as an addition but as an integral part of the tradition. They embody the truth that curanderismo has always been about embracing the whole person, the community, and the earth.

Queer curanderismo is increasingly situated within a global network of gender-diverse spiritual practices, drawing strength from transnational connections. Healers in the Americas have found kinship with practitioners of hijra traditions in South Asia, whose sacred roles as spiritual mediators echo the reverence for gender fluidity found in precolonial curanderismo. Similarly, Two-Spirit traditions in North America and fa'afafine practices in Samoa share a recognition of the sacredness inherent in nonbinary identities. These cross-cultural dialogues not only affirm the universality of queer spiritual roles but also inspire innovation in ritual design. For example, collaborations between Latinx queer curanderes and South Asian healers have led to the blending of Ayurvedic elements, such as turmeric for grounding oneself, with Indigenous herbs like ruda, used for protection. These exchanges reflect the resilience and adaptability of queer healing traditions, forging solidarity across borders and reinforcing the idea that spiritual practices thrive when shared, honored, and reimagined within diverse contexts. The terms *hijra* and *Two-Spirit* are culturally specific and cannot be uncritically applied across contexts. While they offer insights into nonbinary and third-gender roles, their meanings are embedded in distinct colonial, spiritual, and linguistic histories.

This reclamation of queer identities within curanderismo is part of a larger movement toward decolonization. By centering LGBTQ+ voices, queer curanderes challenge the binaries imposed by colonial systems, reclaiming the fluidity and expansiveness of their ancestral traditions. They remind us that healing is inherently intersectional—addressing not only the body and spirit but also the social and historical wounds that shape our lives.

The transnational dimensions of queer curanderismo reveal how spiritual practices thrive through exchange, adaptation, and solidarity across borders. For instance, collaborations between queer curanderes in Latin America and LGBTQ+ healers in the United States illuminate shared struggles against colonial legacies and contemporary marginalization. During a virtual healing summit organized by queer Latinx practitioners in California, participants from Colombia, Mexico, and Brazil shared rituals and techniques that centered around the themes of migration, chosen family, and intersectionality. These exchanges demonstrated not only the adaptability of curanderismo but also its ability to bridge diasporic identities. Similarly, queer curanderas like Luz have drawn parallels between their work and the ancestral healing practices of the Afro-diasporic traditions of Santería and Candomblé, recognizing the interconnected histories of resistance embedded in these practices. By situating queer curanderismo within a global framework, these practitioners challenge the idea of spiritual traditions as static or isolated, emphasizing instead the fluid, evolving nature of healing as an act of global solidarity.

These practices, like queer curanderismo, challenge colonial binaries and celebrate the diversity of human experience. Situating queer curanderismo within a global framework highlights its resonance with other gender-diverse healing traditions worldwide. In Polynesian cultures, the concept of māhū embodies the sacredness of those who bridge male and female energies, reflecting a fluid understanding of gender and spirituality. Similarly, the sworn virgins of the Balkans navigate societal constraints while holding spaces of unique power and identity. These traditions, like queer curanderismo, challenge rigid binaries and celebrate diversity as a sacred force. By connecting their work to this global tapestry, queer curanderes assert that their practices are neither isolated nor anomalous—they are part of a universal movement reclaiming the sacredness of marginalized identities. This perspective strengthens their mission, situating their rituals as acts of solidarity with global struggles for justice, healing, and cultural survival.

Through their activism, rituals, and online platforms, queer curanderes demonstrate that curanderismo is a living tradition, capable of evolving to meet the needs of all who seek its wisdom. In their hands, it continues to thrive, offering healing, hope, and resistance in a world that so often seeks to marginalize. As Marco reflects, "Curanderismo isn't just about keeping our traditions alive—it's about making them a force for justice and liberation."

A TESTIMONIO OF A QUEER CURANDERE: JAVIER'S JOURNEY AS A TWO-SPIRIT HEALER

Javier, a Two-Spirit curandere from New Mexico, reflects on reclaiming ancestral roles once celebrated but marginalized under colonial systems. "Growing up, I felt out of place in my family's stories of curanderas. I was told my queerness was 'not traditional,'" they recall. It was during a trip to Oaxaca, reconnecting with Mixtec elders, that

Javier uncovered a profound truth: queerness was sacred in precolonial healing practices. "They told me, 'You walk between worlds. That is your gift.' It changed everything." Today, Javier's practice focuses on LGBTQ+ clients. They perform limpias infused with affirmations of self-love, incorporating symbols of duality, like copal resin and ruda. "Healing starts with seeing ourselves as whole, even when the world doesn't," they explain. Javier's journey highlights how curanderismo offers a path for queer individuals to reclaim both their identities and the sacred roles of their ancestors.

As Javier's story reminds us, healing is not bound by tradition alone. It evolves, embracing the fluidity of identity and spirit. This fluidity reflects the essence of curanderismo, where the boundaries between past and present, healer and healed, are transcended. The following poem honors this sacred truth, inviting us to reflect on the transformative power of inclusion and self-discovery.

SACRED WITHOUT BORDERS

No somos ni hombre ni mujer,
somos el canto del río bajo la luna,
la raíz que se extiende más allá de las fronteras,
el suspiro de la tierra al renacer.
We are neither man nor woman,
we are the song of the river under the moon,
the root that stretches beyond borders,
the sigh of the earth as it is reborn.

No somos lo que dijeron que seríamos,
somos fuego que arde sin permiso,
las espinas del nopal que protegen el corazón,
las sombras que bailan en los cerros.
We are not what they said we would be,
we are fire that burns without permission,
the spines of the cactus that guard the heart,
the shadows that dance on the hills.

Aquí estamos, completos y rebeldes,
en cada rezo tejemos memoria,
y en cada lágrima sembramos esperanza.
Here we are, whole and defiant,
in every prayer we weave memory,
and in every tear we plant hope.

Somos las manos que no se rinden,
las palabras que rompen silencios,
y los cuerpos que se vuelven templos.
We are the hands that never surrender,
the words that break silences,
and the bodies that become temples.

En los altares de familia escogida,
encendemos velas para los que amamos,
y dejamos flores para los que partieron,
porque nuestro amor siempre vuelve, como la lluvia.
In the altars of chosen family,
we light candles for those we love,
and leave flowers for those who have left,
because our love always returns, like the rain.

Madre Tierra, somos tuyos,
somos tus semillas llevadas por el viento,
tus guerreros que luchan con flores y oraciones,
tus hijes que resisten, que sueñan, que sanan.
Mother Earth, we are yours,
we are your seeds carried by the wind,
your warriors who fight with flowers and prayers,
your children who resist, who dream, who heal.

No somos ramas separadas;
somos un solo árbol creciendo hacia el cielo,
alimentado por raíces que nadie puede cortar,
unidos en la tierra y en el espíritu.
We are not separate branches;

we are one tree growing toward the sky,
fed by roots no one can sever,
united in the earth and in spirit.

• • •

Queer curanderismo is a practice that defies limits, transcends binaries, and flourishes in the spaces where identity meets spirit. It speaks to the resilience and sacredness of those who have been marginalized, affirming that their existence is not an anomaly but a vital thread in the fabric of humanity's collective healing. Through its imagery of roots, altars, and the earth's embrace, it reminds us that the sacred belongs to all who seek it, without restriction or exclusion.

In the hands of queer curanderes, curanderismo becomes not only a tradition preserved but a tradition reimagined—one that celebrates diversity as a source of strength and bridges the gaps left by history's wounds. This closing affirmation calls us to honor the sacred in every life and every story, ensuring that the spirit of curanderismo thrives not just in remembrance but in transformation.

Yet the journey of curanderismo does not end within its traditional or even its contemporary boundaries. As the world grows increasingly interconnected, the practices, philosophies, and spirit of curanderismo transcend geographical and cultural divides. Its essence—rooted in reciprocity, balance, and respect for the sacred—offers insights into global healing paradigms, connecting traditions from South America to Africa, Asia, and beyond. Chapter 9 explores how these principles resonate with global Indigenous practices, reinforcing curanderismo's relevance as a universal framework for healing in the modern world.

As the voices of queer and Two-Spirit curanderes remind us, healing begins with reclaiming the sacred within ourselves. This reclamation, however, is not isolated. Across the globe, Indigenous healing traditions echo this interconnected journey—one that spans continents and unites communities through shared reverence for balance, reciprocity, and ancestral wisdom.

CHAPTER 9

TRANSNATIONAL CURANDERISMO

OPENING INVOCATION

The wind carries whispers,
From mountains crowned with clouds
To valleys rich with life.
Ancestral hands weave threads unseen,
Binding us to the past,
And to each other.

Roots spread deep beneath continents,
Through layers of time and soil.
They drink from the earth's quiet knowing
And bloom in lands far from their birth.

The curandere sings to rivers
That do not know borders,
To skies that hold no flags,
To the earth that cradles us all.

Across waters, across lives,
The sacred whispers remain.
They speak of balance,
Of healing as a circle unbroken.

Each seed planted in foreign soil
Becomes a story of resilience.
Each prayer shared across distance
Finds its way home.

Let us gather where the winds meet,
Where the ocean greets the shore,
To listen, to heal, to remember,
For the sacred belongs to all.

• • •

This poem speaks to the heart of curanderismo's global journey. Though deeply rooted in specific places and traditions, the teachings of curanderismo extend far beyond geographical boundaries. Healing, like the elements, transcends divisions and flows wherever it is needed. The invocation calls us to see curanderismo as both an ancestral practice and a global offering, one that unites people, land, and spirit across the world. This chapter explores how curanderismo's lessons resonate with transnational healing practices, ecological movements, cultural adaptation, and decolonial struggles.

TRANSNATIONAL CURANDERISMO

This chapter explores how immigrant curanderas, by practicing within the diasporic landscapes of the United States—especially places like Los Angeles and Long Beach—fuse ancestral healing traditions from their countries of origin with new cultural influences and community needs. The global relevance of curanderismo has its roots in a history of blending and adaptation. Emerging from the collision of Indigenous, African, and European traditions, curanderismo became a practice of survival during colonization. The forced migration of African peoples brought knowledge of healing plants, spiritual rituals, and cosmological systems, which merged with Indigenous beliefs about balance and reciprocity. Meanwhile, Catholicism introduced prayers, saints, and ceremonies that were adapted into the curandera's toolkit.

This syncretism was not a passive process. Indigenous and African communities actively preserved their sacred knowledge by embedding it in accessible and flexible frameworks. Rituals such as limpias, which cleanse the spirit and body, combine Indigenous cosmologies with Catholic prayers. Herbal remedies draw from both local plants and those brought from across the Atlantic. This blending reflects curanderismo's ability to transform without losing its essence, a characteristic that continues to define its global adaptations today.

As migration patterns shifted in the twentieth and twenty-first centuries, curanderismo began to travel with diasporic communities, reaching places far from its traditional roots. This history of resilience and adaptation provides the foundation for curanderismo's engagement with global healing traditions.

GLOBAL IMPLICATIONS

Curanderismo's principles of healing transcend geographic, cultural, and spiritual boundaries. While curanderismo is deeply rooted in the ancient wisdom of its origins, it is not simply a historical practice—it is a living tradition that evolves and adapts to the needs of modern communities. The movement toward global healing integrates ancestral knowledge with contemporary wellness practices, positioning curanderismo as an enduring force in today's world. At its core, curanderismo emphasizes the interconnectedness of the body, spirit, and environment—values that are reflected in many healing traditions worldwide. As the world becomes more interconnected, the relevance of curanderismo in global contexts grows. This section explores how curanderismo engages with broader healing movements, adapts to contemporary challenges, and offers valuable lessons in ecological, cultural, and spiritual resilience.

Curanderismo mirrors the healing traditions of other Indigenous cultures, offering a lens into its universality. For instance, the sangomas of South Africa use divination and herbs to heal both spiritual and physical ailments, emphasizing ancestral guidance. Likewise, the Māori healers of New Zealand rely on rongoā, traditional herbal medicine, intertwined with spiritual practices honoring Papatūānuku, the earth mother. These shared philosophies reinforce a global understanding of health as holistic, in which healing is inseparable from the land, community, and cosmos. When we compare these traditions, curanderismo's role in global Indigenous resurgence and ecological awareness becomes evident.

One of the key elements of curanderismo that aligns with global healing movements is its holistic approach to wellness. Like many Indigenous and traditional healing systems worldwide, curanderismo recognizes that physical, emotional, and spiritual health are deeply interconnected. This approach is mirrored in the practices of African Ifá, Andean shamanism, and South Asian Ayurveda, which emphasize the balance between the individual and the environment. These systems view healing not as a linear process but as a continuous flow of energy that must be maintained in harmony with the land, the community, and the cosmos.

The shared understanding of the sacredness of plants and natural remedies further underscores the global resonance of curanderismo. Herbal medicine in curanderismo, such as the use of ruda or epazote, is not just about curing illness but also about maintaining spiritual harmony with the environment. This philosophy closely parallels the practices of other healing traditions, such as the use of medicinal plants in African Ifá, where herbs are seen as both medicinal and spiritual allies. These similarities demonstrate that, despite cultural and geographic differences, healing traditions often share a common thread of respect for nature and its healing powers.

In recent years, curanderismo's ecological principles have found renewed relevance in global environmental movements. Curanderismo's focus on sacred reciprocity with the earth is reflected in the growing global movement toward ecological healing and sustainability. Across the world, activists are embracing traditional practices that honor the earth as a living, breathing entity. In curanderismo, plants are seen not only as tools for physical healing but as spiritual beings that offer wisdom and guidance. This view aligns with the practices of permaculture and other sustainable agricultural movements that emphasize a reciprocal relationship with the land.

Curanderas today are at the forefront of eco-spiritual movements, using their knowledge of plants and healing to promote environmental justice. In rural Mexico, curanderas are leading efforts to preserve native plant species and traditional farming practices. In urban centers, curanderismo's teachings on sustainability are being revived in community gardens and grassroots environmental initiatives. This intersection between curanderismo and ecological activism demonstrates how the practice's deep respect for the earth can contribute to broader global efforts to combat climate change and protect biodiversity.

As curanderismo travels across borders, it adapts to the needs of diasporic communities, creating hybrid practices that reflect the realities of migration and cultural exchange. In cities like Los Angeles, London, and Buenos Aires, curanderismo has blended with modern wellness practices such as yoga, mindfulness, and energy healing, creating new forms of spiritual practice that resonate with people of all backgrounds. These adaptations are not a departure from tradition but an evolution of curanderismo's core principles. The practice's flexibility allows it to thrive in diverse settings, providing a space for people to connect with their cultural heritage while also embracing contemporary forms of healing. As curanderismo continues to evolve, it has also embraced the digital world, expanding its reach through virtual rituals, online workshops, and healing circles. In a globalized, digitally connected world, curanderismo flourishes in online spaces, offering healing and connection to people from diverse backgrounds. This virtual exchange ensures that the healing practices of curanderismo remain relevant, accessible, and impactful across geographical boundaries.

The rise of digital platforms has further facilitated the global spread of curanderismo. Through social media, online workshops, and digital healing circles, practitioners are able to share their knowledge and rituals with a worldwide audience. This digital exchange has created a global network of curanderismo practitioners who are connected not only by shared rituals but also by the shared experience of navigating modern life's challenges. The adaptability of curanderismo to the digital age is a testament to its enduring relevance and its ability to evolve with the times.

Another critical aspect of curanderismo's global impact is its alignment with decolonial movements worldwide. As a practice that emerged from Indigenous communities resisting colonization, curanderismo is inherently linked to efforts to reclaim ancestral knowledge and challenge the dominance of Western medical and spiritual systems. This decolonial framework has made curanderismo a key player in global movements that seek to dismantle colonial structures and reclaim Indigenous practices.

Curanderismo's role in decolonial movements is particularly evident in its challenge to Western health-care systems, which often focus solely on the physical body and neglect the spiritual and emotional aspects of healing. Curanderismo, with its emphasis on the interconnectedness of the physical, emotional, and spiritual realms, offers an alternative to the reductionist approaches of Western medicine. This alternative framework resonates with global movements that seek to restore Indigenous health practices and challenge the dominance of Western medical paradigms.

Curanderismo's decolonial ethos also connects it to other global struggles for cultural preservation and self-determination. Healers from different traditions are finding solidarity in their shared resistance to the erasure of their knowledge systems. For example, curanderismo has inspired similar movements in Africa, where traditional healers are reclaiming their practices in the face of Western medical imperialism. In the Andes, Indigenous healers are revitalizing their knowledge of plants and spiritual healing as part of broader efforts to preserve Indigenous cultures and resist the forces of globalization that threaten them.

Through these global connections, curanderismo becomes not just a localized practice but a symbol of broader movements for healing, justice, and cultural resilience. It demonstrates the power of Indigenous knowledge systems to survive and thrive in the face of colonialism, migration, and modernity. As curanderismo continues to adapt and engage with global issues, it offers a powerful example of how ancient wisdom can inform and shape contemporary movements for collective healing. As curanderismo intersects with global struggles for cultural preservation and self-determination, it reclaims ancestral knowledge and continues to empower marginalized communities worldwide.

As curanderismo continues to evolve and adapt, it stands not only as a traditional healing practice but as a living consciousness, ready to address the spiritual, cultural, and ecological challenges of the future. In the next section, we will explore how curanderismo's enduring power as a transformative force offers a vision for healing, not only for individuals but for the global community. Curandere consciousness invites us to reclaim our ancestral wisdom, embrace modern transformation, and connect deeply with the earth and each other, moving beyond borders and divisions.

TESTIMONIO OF A CURANDERE—CARLOS

My name is Carlos, and I am a curandere practicing in the United States. I was born in Oaxaca, a land where the rhythms of nature hum louder than any human voice, and the earth is a constant, nurturing presence. From a young age, I was taught by my grandmother, a curandera, who instilled in me a deep reverence for the sacred power of the earth. Her hands would move gently over the plants, selecting those with the deepest medicines, and she would speak to them softly—reminding me that every herb, every flower, had a story to tell, a lesson to impart. She always said, "The earth provides, the plants know, and it is through them that we heal."

Growing up in Oaxaca, I learned that healing was not just about physical remedies. It was about the connection to the land, the spirits, and the community. My grandmother's teachings were clear: curanderismo is a spiritual practice as much as it is a medicinal one, rooted in a profound relationship with nature and a deep respect for the wisdom that has been passed down through generations.

However, when I moved to the United States, everything shifted. The transition from Oaxaca's open spaces, where the mountains and the rivers were part of my daily life, to the busy streets of Los Angeles was a stark contrast. The landscape was unfamiliar, and the connection I once had with the land seemed far away. Yet I carried my grandmother's teachings with me, and soon I discovered that curanderismo, like the plants, was not confined to one place or one time. It adapted. It grew. It was as resilient as the people who practice it.

In the early days of my time in the United States I found it difficult to connect with the land here. I longed for the albahaca (basil) that grew wild in Oaxaca, the epazote that my grandmother used for purification, and the ruda (rue) that protected our family. I felt disconnected from the familiar plants, unsure of where to begin. But soon I realized that the healing practice of curanderismo could be both deeply rooted in tradition and expansive in its reach. The herbs may have been different, but the spirit of curanderismo remained the same.

I began working with the plants that were available to me here—cedar for protection, rosemary for clarity, and sage for purification. Each new plant I encountered became a teacher, just as my grandmother had taught me to see the spirit in every herb, every tree. The same principles applied: healing was about listening—to the plants, to the earth, to the spirits—and adapting to the landscape, while still honoring the teachings passed down to me from Oaxaca.

One of the rituals I developed in my new home is the limpia de conexión. This ritual is a powerful healing practice I use to send healing energy across great distances. Whether someone is in Mexico, the United States, or halfway around the world, this ritual connects us through the energy of the plants, my intention, and the spirit world. It transcends time and space—just as curanderismo itself transcends borders and is rooted in a tradition that connects us all.

The ritual begins with the preparation of an herbal tea. I carefully select herbs with healing intentions. Ruda (rue) for purification, epazote for protection, basil for strength, and cedar for grounding. These herbs, though they may grow in different soils from the ones in Oaxaca, carry the same energy: an energy of healing that flows through generations and across continents.

As I steep the herbs in boiling water, I sit quietly with the cup, offering a prayer of intention. I call upon the spirit of the person I am healing, speaking their name aloud and inviting their energy into the space. The herbs infuse the water with their sacred energy. The steam rising from the cup is not just water—it is a bridge, carrying my thoughts and prayers across time and space. Through this simple tea, I send my intention to them—across oceans, across borders, across the distance.

As the steam rises from the tea, I focus on the connection between us. Though we may be miles apart, I know that the spirit of curanderismo, like the plants, knows no boundaries. The steam, carrying the healing energy of the plants, becomes the medium through which I send my prayers. It's as if we are no longer separated by distance; instead, we are connected through the ritual, through the shared energy of the plants, and through our collective intention.

Once the tea is ready, I bless it with gratitude. I offer thanks to the plants for their wisdom, for their sacred healing, and for the spirits who guide my work. I send the healing energy out into the world, trusting that it will reach the person I have worked for, whether they are in the United States, in Mexico, or anywhere else on this earth. I know that the plants I have worked with carry the wisdom of Oaxaca, and they also carry the wisdom of every healer who has ever used them to heal. This is the power of curanderismo—it is not confined to one place, one person, or one time.

In performing the limpia de conexión, I am reminded that curanderismo is a transnational practice. It is both deeply local and profoundly global. It carries with it the teachings of my grandmother, the earth of Oaxaca, and the energy of the world around us. Curanderismo, like the plants, is always adapting, always connecting, always reaching across the distance to heal. It is not just about the herbs or the rituals—it is about the connection we share as people and as healers, across all borders.

GLOBAL INDIGENOUS HEALING

In South Africa, sangomas—traditional healers of the Zulu and Xhosa peoples—offer a parallel to curanderismo. Like curanderas, sangomas communicate with ancestors through divination, herbal remedies, and ceremonial dances. Their use of medicinal plants such as imphepho, a sacred herb for cleansing and invocation, mirrors the role of ruda in limpias. As one sangoma explains, "Healing is not just about the body; it is about the spirit and the land." This resonance between curanderismo and African traditions underscores a shared global understanding: healing requires harmony between the physical, spiritual, and ecological realms. These cross-cultural parallels reveal the universality of ancestral wisdom, connecting curanderismo to a broader tapestry of global Indigenous healing practices.

In Bali, healers practice a spiritual medicine rooted in balance, much like curanderismo. Using purification rituals involving water temples and offerings of flowers and rice, Balinese healers seek harmony between the seen (sekala) and unseen (niskala) worlds. This duality mirrors the curandere's approach, in which physical and spiritual dimensions intertwine to heal the whole being. As one balian explains, "We heal not only the person but their relationship to the cosmos." Such parallels remind us that Indigenous healing practices worldwide share common values, even as they adapt to their unique cultural and environmental contexts.

In Hawai'i, practitioners of ho'oponopono—a traditional method of conflict resolution and healing—emphasize restoring harmony within the individual, the family, and the community. Rooted in the Hawaiian cosmology of interconnectedness, ho'oponopono often involves prayers, chants, and discussions mediated by a kahu (spiritual leader). Similar to curanderismo's focus on reciprocity and cleansing, ho'oponopono addresses spiritual imbalances to realign relationships. As kahu Charles explains, "Healing begins when we recognize our shared breath with the world—our aloha." Such practices remind us that the essence of healing transcends geography, resonating across Indigenous traditions worldwide.

These shared principles—of balance, community, and spiritual reciprocity—underscore the universality of Indigenous healing traditions, reminding us that curanderismo is part of a much larger global mosaic.

MARÍA KIM'S FUSION HEALING PRACTICE

María Kim, a practitioner based in Los Angeles, integrates curanderismo with Korean shamanic traditions. Raised by a Mexican mother and a Korean father, María grew up immersed in two distinct yet mutually resonant healing philosophies. "Curanderismo taught me que las plantas tienen sabiduría," she explains, her Spanish accent blending seamlessly with her Korean heritage. "And my halmeoni—my Korean grandmother—showed me how to honor ancestors through ritual."

María's fusion practice combines elements of both traditions. She performs limpias while offering bowls of rice and incense to honor both ancestral lines. "Es sobre equilibrio—it's about balance," she says. María's practice often begins with a Korean ritual of bowing to ancestors, followed by a limpia that draws on her Mexican heritage. "It's like weaving un tejido—a fabric," she explains. "Every thread, whether it's copal or incense, connects me to both my lineages." This approach allows her clients to experience a healing process that honors the interconnectedness of multiple cultural traditions. "In Korean shamanism, we call it 'han,' a sense of interconnected sorrow and healing. En curanderismo, es igual—honoring what connects us while releasing what holds us back." Her work demonstrates how curanderismo's principles adapt to cross-cultural contexts, creating bridges between traditions and expanding its reach as a universal framework for healing.

The testimonios in this chapter affirm that curanderismo in the United States is not practiced in isolation, but rather in dialogue with migration, memory, and place. Healers such as Carlos, who is Oaxaqueño and now lives in the United States, and María Kim, who brings together Korean shamanic traditions and Mexican curanderismo in Los Angeles, exemplify how immigrant curanderas/os/es contribute to the transformation and enrichment of local healing practices. Rather than treating curanderismo as a static or nationally bound tradition, these practitioners create a living archive of transnational, multiracial, and diasporic medicine. In places like Los Angeles and Long Beach—where immigrant communities from across the world intersect—curanderismo becomes a space of cultural fusion and innovation. The spiritual technologies these healers carry are not only remembered but reactivated and reshaped through everyday encounters, digital connections, and cross-cultural kinship. In this way, curanderismo in the United States becomes a mirror of migration itself: layered, adaptive, rooted, and transformative.

CANTOS DE LA TIERRA

Through los ríos, and across el cielo,
whispers de sanación float in the viento.
Una voz rises en las alas del humo,
anciana como las montañas, pero siempre nueva.

From the alma of the earth, las raíces crecen,
entrelazándose beneath oceans y bajo el tiempo.
El espíritu de las plantas atraviesa fronteras,

bringing stories no contadas, sangre y tierra,
carried by those que escuchan with hearts open.

La curandera speaks—not with words alone,
pero con la fuerza of the stars, el corazón de la tierra,
moviendo montañas with her hands,
carrying las oraciones de los que vinieron antes,
and la tierra responds,
suave y eterna como el sol,
susurrando nuestros nombres in every breath.

Even when bodies are separados by distancia,
caminamos juntos—unidos by the song del viento,
el grito of our ancestors—
you y yo, connected by the same heartbeat
that beats in cada planta, in cada hoja,
in every lágrima caída.

The humo rises—sagrado, profundo,
lleno de memoria, de vida, de transformación.
Crossing oceans y montañas,
healing us all, un baile circular
of esperanza y renacimiento.

And when las plantas speak, we know—
somos uno—siempre,
through la tierra, through las plantas,
through the silencio que llena los espacios entre nosotros,
beyond time, beyond borders,
we are whole again.

• • •

This poem is not just a prayer of healing—it is a reflection of the spirit that moves across time and space. Curanderismo, like the earth, is vast and ever-changing, yet it is always deeply rooted in the wisdom of those who came before us. Through the smoke, through the plants, and through the voices of our ancestors, we find our way back to the sacred circle of life. In the distance between us, across borders and boundaries, the healing power of curanderismo reaches beyond the physical. It speaks in whispers, in the language of the earth, of connection, of memory. It is a practice that transcends geography, that connects us all—whether we are in the hills of Oaxaca, the streets of Los Angeles, or the corners of the world we have yet to touch.

Curanderismo is a living, breathing force. It evolves with the land, the people, and the time. Yet at its heart it remains the same: a sacred relationship with the earth, the plants, and each other. It is a call to listen, to heal, and to remember the ties that bind us, not just to our ancestors but to the world around us. This poem is a reminder that we are one—always, in the soil, in the plants, in the smoke that rises and the breath we share. And as we heal, we pass this wisdom forward, carrying it across the distance, bridging the spaces between us, so that the spirit of curanderismo can continue to grow, to heal, and to unite.

As we have seen, curanderismo transcends borders, evolving and adapting across cultures while staying deeply rooted in the wisdom of the land. Its ability to bridge the physical and spiritual realms, to heal across distances, speaks to the enduring power of ancestral knowledge in an increasingly interconnected world. But while curanderismo continues to adapt and expand, it remains a practice that calls us back to our origins—the earth, the plants, the community. In the closing chapter, we turn to the transformative nature of curanderismo, reflecting on its role as a living consciousness—a consciousness that calls on us to remember, reclaim, and heal. Curandere consciousness offers a vision for the future, one that embraces both the ancient and the contemporary, the local and the global, inviting us to connect with the world around us and with the deeper truths that guide our shared humanity.

CLOSING

Curandere Consciousness

Healing begins with a whisper—a quiet call to remember. It is the breath of the earth, the song of the ancestors, and the pulse of the community. Curanderismo, at its heart, is a tradition of remembrance. It reminds us of our place in the sacred web of life, where every plant, every story, and every prayer is a thread that binds us together.

Throughout this book, we have journeyed through the rich tapestry of curanderismo. We have walked alongside urban curanderas transforming concrete jungles into sanctuaries of healing. We have celebrated the courage of queer healers reclaiming spaces erased by colonial forces. We have traveled across oceans and time, witnessing as curanderismo adapts, thrives, and connects us in ways that transcend borders. At every turn, this tradition has shown its profound resilience, its capacity to heal not only individuals but entire communities and ecosystems.

Curanderismo is a consciousness—a way of seeing, living, and being that honors the interconnectedness of all things. In an era marked by fragmentation, it calls us back to wholeness. It teaches us to see the earth as a living entity, to treat healing as a sacred act of reciprocity, and to listen deeply to the wisdom of the plants, the spirits, and our ancestors. It is both a resistance to forces that seek to divide us and a reclamation of our sacred inheritance.

As we look toward the future, curanderismo holds a powerful vision for healing the world. In the face of climate crisis, it reminds us of our responsibility to the earth. In moments of cultural erasure, it guides us to reclaim and celebrate our roots. In a time of spiritual disconnection, it offers rituals and practices that ground us in the sacred. This tradition, shaped by centuries of survival and adaptation, continues to evolve, weaving its wisdom into modern contexts and global movements.

But curanderismo is not a relic of the past—it is alive, breathing in the gardens we grow, the stories we tell, and the prayers we share. It asks us to carry its wisdom forward, not as practitioners limited by tradition but as co-creators of a healing legacy that bridges the ancient and the contemporary. In embodying curandere consciousness, we honor the land, the ancestors, and each other. We become the keepers of a flame that lights the way for generations to come.

Curanderismo asks us to be not just practitioners but protectors—guardians of its sacred truths, its connection to the earth, and its gifts to our communities. In protecting this legacy, we ensure it continues to thrive, weaving its healing spirit into the fabric of a more balanced, compassionate world.

In the spirit of the curandere, we are called to nurture the seeds of resilience planted by those who came before us. To tend not only the gardens of the earth but the gardens of identity, memory, and belonging. Whether through reclaiming our sacred histories, standing in solidarity with marginalized voices, or protecting the land that sustains us, we become vessels for the sacred, weaving together ancient wisdom and contemporary purpose.

Curanderismo evolves not only in its rituals but in its language, its art, and even its adaptation to digital spaces, where healers and communities now gather to share their wisdom. This adaptability ensures that its sacred threads remain vibrant and unbroken, ready to meet the needs of a changing world. The consciousness of the curandere reminds us that healing is a dynamic process, rooted in reciprocity, guided by spirit, and open to new possibilities.

As you close this book, reflect on the curanderismo within you—your connection to the earth, your ancestors, and your community. The practices described here are not relics; they are alive, waiting to be nurtured and reimagined. In carrying forward this sacred lineage, we collectively weave the fabric of healing and resilience for future generations.

EL CÍRCULO SAGRADO

In the viento, susurros rise,
memorias carved en piedra y fuego.
Hands that built pyramids,
that healed tierras broken por conquista,
still guide us.

El humo lifts our prayers al cielo,
carrying siglos of voices—
abuelas que nunca dejaron de cantar,
niños who carry semillas en sus bolsillos,
waiting for tierra that welcomes them home.

Roots dig deep, atravesando fronteras,
sipping la sangre of generations.
Cada planta, un maestro; cada hoja, un verso,
writing historias de sanación y resistencia.

The sun burns bright—recordándonos,
healing belongs to those who remember.
The moon cradles los secretos del río,
reflecting caminos perdidos, now reclaimed.

Somos guardianes de lo sagrado.
In cada limpia, in cada palabra susurrada al viento,
we stitch together worlds shattered by olvido.
The earth, nuestra madre,
sings en lenguas we are learning to love again.

In la danza of healing, somos uno:
en el humo, en la tierra, en las estrellas que nos guían.
El fuego dentro enciende el recuerdo.
The agua purifies lo perdido, lo quebrado.

From Oaxaca's mountains to LA's calles,
from the Andes to el Bronx,
curanderismo calls us to return—
to reclaim, resist, y sanar juntos.

Somos raíces—strong, braided with fuerza,
stretching across océanos y siglos.
Somos el tambor, el canto, el grito,
a breath that shakes montañas,
a fire that dances en la oscuridad.
El círculo sagrado nos llama siempre—
unbroken, eternal, transforming,
echoing in cada latido del corazón,
binding us to what was, and to all that will be.

• • •

As we step into this consciousness, we are called to action—not only to honor these traditions but to live them. To plant the seeds of healing in our communities. To listen to the wisdom of the earth and our ancestors. To create spaces where stories, rituals, and lives flourish in the face of adversity. Curanderismo asks us to be not just practitioners but protectors, weaving its sacred threads into the fabric of a more balanced, compassionate world.

As we conclude this journey, we return to the spirit invoked at the beginning of this book: the curandere as a bridge between worlds, traditions, and futures. Their wisdom—rooted in the past yet open to the horizons of tomorrow—reminds us that healing is both an act of transformation and a commitment to connection. Through their practices, they weave a tapestry of resilience and reciprocity, carrying forward the sacred threads that unite us all.

How will you carry forward this legacy of healing in your own life? The curandera calls to all of us, not as a distant figure but as a reminder of what we can reclaim and reimagine.

ACKNOWLEDGMENTS

This book emerged through relationships, care, and lineages of knowledge that extend far beyond me. *Curandereando* was shaped by ancestral memory, community wisdom, and collective acts of healing that cannot be contained within a single author's name.

I am grateful to the editors, reviewers, and production team at the University of Arizona Press for their thoughtful engagement with this manuscript. I offer particular thanks to Kristen Buckles, acquisitions editor, for her guidance, support, and belief in this project from its earliest stages. I am also thankful to Matt Gleeson for his careful reading and editorial insight, which helped sharpen the manuscript while respecting its decolonial and relational commitments.

I extend deep gratitude to Martha Gonzalez and Enrique C. Ochoa, whose contributions to this book are both intellectual and visionary. Martha Gonzalez's prefatory invocación and Enrique C. Ochoa's foreword frame this work with political clarity, historical depth, and profound care for community-based knowledge. Their scholarship and generosity shaped how this book speaks to the world.

This book is an offering to my mother, Eva Cupchoy. Long before I had language for curanderismo, I learned it through her hands, her remedies, and her quiet knowing. The ideas that became *Curandereando* were born from honoring her healing practices and the maternal wisdom she carries. I also honor my grandmothers, whose presence continues to guide this work in spirit. Their ways of knowing, healing, and surviving live on through memory, prayer, and practice, and their wisdom moves through these pages as an ancestral force. Together, they form the living and ancestral foundation from which this book grew.

I offer my deepest gratitude to the individuals who entrusted me with their testimonios and oral histories. Their generosity, courage, and care made this book possible. Through their lived experiences, these pages reflect the many ways curanderismo continues to thrive, adapt, and endure across communities, generations, and geographies, and I hope their stories inspire others to one day speak their own truths and experiences with curanderismo. I hold these stories with deep responsibility and respect.

Finally, I acknowledge the ancestors and the land that hold this work. This book was written in dialogue with place, memory, and spirit, and it carries forward the enduring labor of healing, resistance, and remembrance.

GLOSSARY

Ajq'ijab: Maya spiritual guides who serve as timekeepers and healers within the sacred Tzolk'in calendar.

Altar: A sacred space where curanderas and curanderos place offerings, herbs, and symbolic items to connect with spiritual energies.

Balian: Traditional healers from Bali who integrate spiritual purification rituals with offerings to harmonize the seen (sekala) and unseen (niskala) worlds.

Borderlands: A concept theorized by Gloria Anzaldúa to describe the liminal space between multiple cultural, national, and spiritual worlds, particularly as experienced by Chicanx and Indigenous peoples living along the U.S.-Mexico border. It is both a geopolitical and a metaphysical space of tension, creativity, and resistance.

Bruja/Brujo/Bruje: Terms referring to a witch or healer. Historically used pejoratively but reclaimed as an empowering identity by some practitioners.

Chachawarmi: A Quechua concept representing balance and reciprocity in relationships, both human and cosmic.

Copal: Resin burned during rituals to cleanse spaces and elevate prayers to the divine.

Curandera/o/e: Traditional healer specializing in spiritual, physical, and emotional healing. The gender-neutral term *curandere* reflects inclusivity in modern practices.

Curanderismo: A traditional Latin American healing system blending Indigenous, African, and European influences.

Danza de los Voladores: A ritual dance of the Totonac people, symbolizing spiritual connection through a performance involving flying.

Epazote: A medicinal herb used in spiritual cleansings and physical remedies.

Ho'oponopono: A Hawaiian practice of reconciliation and healing, emphasizing communal and spiritual harmony.

Limpia: A cleansing ritual designed to remove negative energies and restore harmony to the spirit and body.

Medicinal Gardens: Spaces where plants with healing properties are cultivated, reflecting the reciprocal relationship between curanderas and the land.

Nepantla: A Nahuatl term describing the in-between state of transition, often used to explore cultural hybridity and spiritual transformation.

Pachamama: The Andean earth goddess, symbolizing the interconnectedness of life and the sacred reciprocity between humans and nature.

Pulque: A traditional Mexican beverage made from the fermented sap of the maguey (agave) plant. Pulque has been consumed since pre-Columbian times and holds cultural and spiritual significance, often used in rituals and ceremonies to honor deities and connect with the spiritual world.

Ruda (Rue): A sacred herb used for protection and spiritual cleansing in curanderismo.

Sangomas: Healers of the Zulu and Xhosa people in South Africa who use divination and herbal medicine to connect with ancestors and restore balance.

Tonantzin: An Aztec goddess representing motherhood and the earth, often syncretized with the Virgin of Guadalupe.

Two-Spirit: A term used by some Indigenous North American communities to describe gender-diverse individuals who embody both masculine and feminine spirits.

BIBLIOGRAPHY

Archives

Archivo General de Centroamérica. Guatemala City, Guatemala. [Contains historical records related to Maya healing practices labeled as idolatry.]
Archivo General de Indias. Seville, Spain. [Contains reports on Andean healing rituals during Spanish colonization.]
Archivo General de la Nación. Mexico City, Mexico. [Contains records documenting colonial curanderismo practices, including cases of spiritual healing accused of being witchcraft.]
Museo Nacional de Antropología. Mexico City, Mexico.

Testimonios

The following individuals shared their oral histories and testimonios, contributing to the collective understanding of curanderismo. In this book, testimonios encompass both direct, lived accounts and composite narratives that are based on rigorous research, archival records, and oral traditions. Only first names are used to protect the privacy of contributors while honoring the deeply personal and sacred nature of their stories. Interviews were conducted in community settings in Los Angeles, California, and various regions in Mexico, capturing the cultural and environmental contexts that shape these narratives. Composite testimonios draw from historical fragments, oral histories, and ethnographic studies, ensuring they are firmly rooted in the lived realities and spiritual practices of curanderas across time and space. Together, these testimonios illuminate the lives, resilience, and traditions of curanderas, reminding us that their healing practices are not just acts of personal care but also collective, ancestral, and revolutionary processes of resistance and reclamation. The testimonios include those of:

Alejandro
Alex
Ana Lluvia
Berna
Carlos
Charles
Christian
Clara
Doña Carmen
Doña Esperanza
Elena
Eli
Erika Buenaflor
Esperanza
Hijra
Ixtoii Paloma Cervantes
Iztli
Jaime
Javier
José Esteban Muñoz
Lucía
Luz
Marco
María Kim
María Luz
Marisol
Mateo
Rosa
Sofía
Xochitl
Yadira Marie

Secondary Sources

Anzaldúa, Gloria E. *Borderlands / La Frontera: The New Mestiza*. Aunt Lute Books, 1987.

Bussmann, Rainer W. "The Globalization of Traditional Medicine in Northern Peru." *Evidence-Based Complementary and Alternative Medicine*, December 28, 2013, article ID 291903. https://doi.org/10.1155/2013/291903.

Butler, Judith. *Gender Trouble: Feminism and the Subversion of Identity*. Routledge, 1990.

Cáceres, Berta. "Acceptance Speech, 2015 Goldman Prize Ceremony." YouTube video, 3:19, uploaded April 22, 2015, by Goldman Environmental Prize. https://www.youtube.com/watch?v=AR1kwx8b0ms&t=42s.

Cisneros, Sandra. *Woman Hollering Creek*. Vintage Contemporaries, 1991.

Delgadillo, Theresa. *Spiritual Mestizaje: Religion, Gender, Race, and Nation in Contemporary Chicana Narrative*. Duke University Press, 2011.

Gonzales, Patrisia. *Red Medicine: Traditional Indigenous Rites of Birthing and Healing*. University of Arizona Press, 2012.

Hagler, Anderson. "Excesses of Religion: Indigenous and African Descent Peoples, Catholicism, and the Management of the Supernatural in Colonial Mexico." PhD diss., Duke University, 2021.

Hendrickson, Brett. "Curanderismo in the Americas." In *The Routledge Handbook of Religion, Medicine, and Health*, edited by Dorothea Lüddeckens, Philipp Hetmanczyk, Pamela E. Klassen, and Justin B. Stein, 41–53. Routledge, 2024.

Levins Morales, Aurora. *Medicine Stories: Essays for Radicals*. South End Press, 1998.

Lugones, María. "Heterosexualism and the Colonial/Modern Gender System." *Hypatia* 22, no. 1 (2007): 186–209.

Moraga, Cherríe L. *Loving in the War Years*. South End Press, 1983.

Perez, Maria Esmeralda. "Curanderismo and Healing Rituals: An Ethnographic and Historical Study of the Casma Valley in Northern Peru." Master's thesis, University of Texas Rio Grande Valley, 2022.

Polanco, Edward Anthony. *Healing Like Our Ancestors: The Nahua Tiçitl, Gender, and Settler Colonialism in Central Mexico, 1535–1660*. University of Arizona Press, 2024.

Torres, Eliseo "Cheo". *Curandero: A Life in Mexican Folk Healing*. University of New Mexico Press, 1998.

INDEX

ABOUT THE AUTHOR

Lani Cupchoy is a public historian, storyteller, artivista, and filmmaker of Chicana, Afro-indígena, Kānaka Maoli, and Chinese heritage. She teaches in the Department of Chicana/o and Latina/o Studies at California State University, Los Angeles, specializing in public history, ethnic studies, and Indigenous knowledge. Founder of Pinkjade Creations, she uses film, music, and digital media to amplify testimonios and cultural resilience. Her work bridges scholarship, ancestral healing traditions, and community-engaged storytelling.

Printed and bound by CPI Group (UK) Ltd, Croydon, CR0 4YY

13/08/2026

14941844-0008